VIRTUAL BOSS

A practical guide for masterfully leading and managing remote teams

RALPH BURNS

This publication is designed to provide accurate and authoritative information in regard to the subject matter covered. It is sold with the understanding that neither the author nor the publisher is engaged in rendering legal, accounting, or other professional service. If legal advice or other expert assistance is required, the services of a competent professional person should be sought.

Published in the USA
tiereleven.com

Printed in the USA

First Edition

ISBN: 978-0-578-90377-4

Cover and Interior Design: Swish Publishing

To my dad who helped inspire me to become an entrepreneur, urged me to always be myself, and persistently nudged me to unleash my creativity on the world.

And to my wife Jennifer for empowering me to chase my dreams and giving me the never-ending confidence and courage to succeed.

CONTENTS

INTRODUCTION

When Mason first arrived at my company, Tier 11, as the new Director of Operations, he was making a jump that will likely resonate with most readers of this book—he went from managing a single employee, to managing a virtual team of nearly twenty people.

After many sixty-plus hour weeks in the role, he found himself frustrated and dead tired. Mason's natural management style was the 'nice guy boss'. But he was quickly finding that, while this was an approach he could get away with if he only had a few direct reports in a physical office, it was completely impractical for a virtual management role. His new role was one that involved guiding a group of inexperienced managers who were leading their own teams of customer-facing workers, many of whom were not performing to expectations.

Not only was Mason required to coach and lead his management team, but he often had to step in and deal with the underperforming workers directly. All of which had to be done from behind his computer screen. Adding to the mounting pressure was the awkward fact that he was now leading and managing people who only weeks prior had been his co-workers.

Eva's ascension in my company was slightly different from Mason's. She had worked her way up from being a frontline employee through to a number of other managerial roles before being promoted to Vice President of her division. This new role gave her responsibility for three managers as well as several frontline employees of her own.

Until that most recent promotion to VP, Eva's management style was one where she did all the thinking for the people in her teams and then passed things over to them to handle the necessary execution. All of her previous management experience involved overseeing a few employees in a physical location, but now she found herself managing a remote team of nearly a dozen frontline workers.

She'd never needed to train or coach her previous employees because the relationship was very much one of, "Here's what I need you to do. Once you do it, I can then see how you're doing it." This worked out fine when she was responsible for the output and performance of a relatively small number of people, but once she became the Virtual Boss of a team of over twenty people, her strategy was far less effective.

Suffice to say, Mason and Eva's lack of experience in leading teams created several challenges for them. As someone who'd been managing remote sales teams for over twenty years, I recognized their struggles immediately.

Those struggles could be boiled down to:

1. How do I get top-tier performance out of my people?

2. More importantly, how do I get top-tier performance out of my people when *I don't see them every single day?*

These challenges were ones I'd had to overcome in my own career on the way to winning dozens of individual company awards, team awards, and handfuls of national sales awards as both an individual and a team leader.

Most importantly, they were the very same challenges I had to overcome in turning Tier 11 into an eight-figure virtual business.

Through the use of trial and error as well as knowledge of what worked for me as a sales professional, sales manager, sales director and now three-time CEO, I built what I called The Virtual Boss System™—a set of systems and processes that helped me become a highly effective remote leader.

And it's a system that will work for you to do the very same.

A highly effective Virtual Boss must have these characteristics:

- The trust of the people on their team
- Teams that consistently perform above expectations
- The ability to challenge and draw the best out of everyone
- The ability to set a tone of excellence that permeates throughout the entire organization
- A willingness to keep learning and evolving

Having my own business and witnessing leaders like Mason and Eva struggling with aspects of managing their respective virtual teams was the genesis of The Virtual Boss System™. I was curious to see if the systems and strategies I'd developed for myself could be taught to others to help them become better leaders and managers.

Initially, Mason found it hard to get the best out of his team. When managing his teams, he would jump to conclusions and make potentially hurtful assumptions, especially with regard to the underperformers. Like most virtual managers, he often wrongfully assumed that because he couldn't physically *see* them working, that they were not. His team eventually picked up on this and it subsequently created an environment of mistrust and underperformance.

Mason didn't start achieving success until he fully implemented The Virtual Boss System™.

Here's what he had to say about it:

> When I first started with Tier 11, I had very little experience in coaching and leadership, let alone doing it remotely. I was coming from an environment where I was the one doing a lot of the actual work with the help of a few other employees. Now I was in the position of getting results through others, managing other people to do the work, and needing to demonstrate a result.
>
> I was also having to deal with underperformers. When you're dealing with underperformers in a virtual environment, it's easy to jump to conclusions and make assumptions when people go missing or aren't getting the job done. Happily for me, I had Ralph's Virtual Boss System™ to help and he was able to go way beyond simply providing advice and guidance—he had clear strategies for dealing with every situation I faced.
>
> Take the case of one underperformer (who I will call John).

Instead of making assumptions, I used The Virtual Boss System™ to communicate effectively with John and together we laid the problem out on the table really clearly. From there, John and I were able to put together a very clear plan and agreement on how we were going to measure success from that point on. Once that was done, it was just about holding John accountable to executing that plan.

The Virtual Boss System™ gave me a lot of confidence as a manager and helped John improve his performance. It also helped John feel confident that I had his back because I was showing up with tools that could help resolve the situation, rather than just coming down hard on him. And of course, me being a better manager helped Tier 11 as a business to achieve its goals.

Today, I'm now a manager of managers—someone who's able to help other managers in this business implement the systems Ralph gave me to achieve great success as Virtual Bosses.

How did Eva put the system to use?

Remember, she was someone who wanted to do it all for her team, but knew she could never scale her influence unless she changed her approach. Like many bosses, she was also unsure how to motivate and lead when things weren't going well.

Here's what she had to say:

When I started working for Tier 11, I had some bad management habits to break! I tended to want to do it all for my team, as I thought it was just plain faster than coaching them on how to think and do it for themselves. I was also unsure how to turn people's performance around when things weren't going well, and how to manage people who weren't meeting expectations.

The Virtual Boss System™ was integral in giving me the confidence required to get effective results through the work of others: delegating effectively and giving others the skills to be able to get results on their own—instead of me always being the one to do or initiate everything and fix their problems.

The Virtual Boss System™ walked me through the process of asking better questions of my team so as to assist them in finding solutions themselves, not me always having to find the solutions for them. This was a MAJOR shift in my thinking. It also showed me how to communicate just the right amount of info as well as to accept that an uncomfortable silence is OK; I don't always have to fill the silence with chatter!

Where The Virtual Boss System™ came in most useful for me, however, was in managing my own underperformer (who I'll call Brian). I realized Brian was struggling to cope with the account he currently had and that we needed to move him onto a 'simpler' account. This would give him the training he needed to get better while being less risky for us. Knowing that he would be disappointed by being taken off the account,

I used scripts from The Virtual Boss System™ to help me convey to Brian that his skill set would be better matched with a different customer because his current situation was setting him up for failure. It was amazing to see how addressing this issue in a positive light for Brian turned what could have been a demoralizing situation into a very positive one.

Instead of always being the one to do everything, Eva simply needed the confidence to delegate effectively and empower her team to get results on their own. In doing so, she also learned to trust her team to get the job done, no matter what continent they were on or what time zone they were in.

Mason and Eva weren't the only people in my organization who benefited from The Virtual Boss System™. I taught this system to my entire management team and the effect on Tier 11's results have been nothing short of remarkable. In less than seven years, this system has helped Tier 11 grow from being just a two-person team to a virtual workforce of over fifty people in over twenty countries and six continents.

ABOUT THIS BOOK

I know there are many Virtual Bosses out there. If you're reading this book, you're one of them. The experience I had teaching my team the leadership systems and strategies I've developed over the years has shown quite clearly that those things aren't just something that works for me—they will work for anyone. Including you.

All of which brings me to the purpose of this book. What I've done here is codify and simplify everything I've learned over twenty years of managing to achieve extremely high levels of performance. Whether you're managing a small team of remote workers within a Fortune 500 company or building an eight-figure virtual business from scratch with over fifty workers on six continents, this simple system will work for you. Additionally, the material contained here has also been used to train our internal management team at Tier 11 and has also enabled us to double in size each year for the past seven years, while managing a digital advertising portfolio of over $100 million.

The teachings are divided into five easy sections:

- **SECTION 1:** Unlocking the potential of your remote staff by making regular "trust deposits" into their personal "Trust Accounts"

- **SECTION 2:** Setting the bar "higher" (not just "high")
- **SECTION 3:** Motivating your team to achieve peak performance
- **SECTION 4:** Leading your team to rockstar status
- **SECTION 5:** Turning around underperforming staff in 30 days

The great thing about this book is that while I certainly recommend reading it from start to finish to get the full picture, you can skip straight to the section that best fits your current needs.

So, if you have a specific need, skip straight to that section now. If you don't need to head straight there, however, happy days! Turn the page and let's talk about the most important ingredient in unlocking the potential of your virtual team ... loading up deposits in the Trust Account.

SECTION 1

UNLEASH THE BEST BY MAKING DEPOSITS IN THE TRUST ACCOUNT

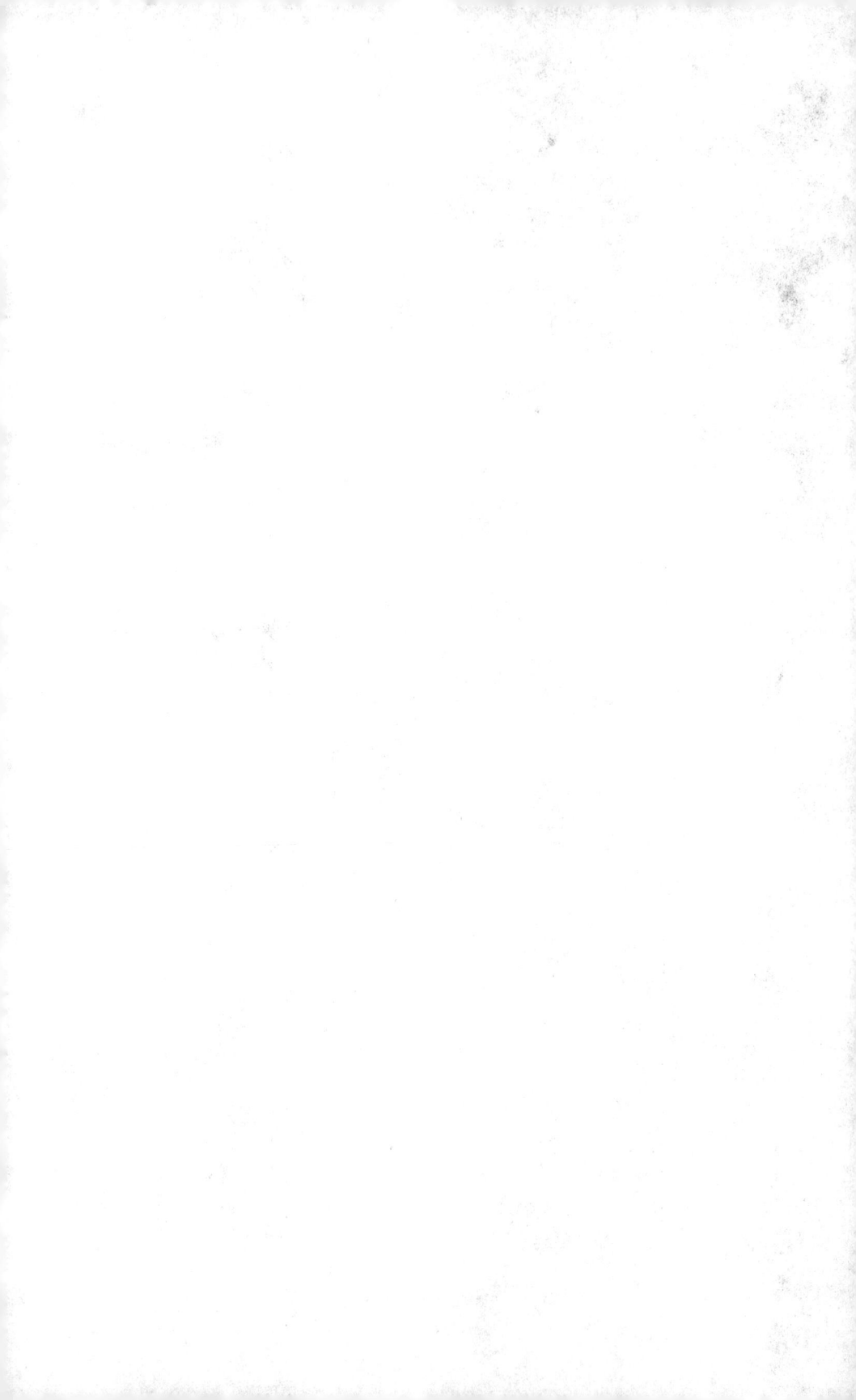

UNLEASH THE BEST BY MAKING DEPOSITS IN THE TRUST ACCOUNT

Conventional wisdom has it all wrong. Conventional wisdom dictates that a manager should treat all their staff the same.

"Be fair," it says, "don't play favorites."

The Golden Rule says "treat others the way that you would like to be treated." Follow this and you'll never go wrong (says conventional wisdom).

None of this works in the virtual management world, however.

If you "treat others the way that you would like to be treated," that means they're exactly like you. Furthermore, if you treat every staff member the same way, this suggests that they are all the same.

Are they? You know better than that.

Every staff member has a different set of motivations, fears, idiosyncrasies, talents, and drives. If you can:

- uncover the hidden inner workings of your staff;

- use those facts to guide all your interactions with them; and

- speak to them in terms of what is important to them

then you'll be far ahead of the rest of all the other Virtual Bosses out there.

I will say, however, that while the "Golden Rule" doesn't apply when it comes to motivating and leading, it DOES apply when it comes to trusting. The one thing that is universal is trust. You need to look for ways to strengthen your staff's trust in you at every turn and every possible moment.

Once you get that trust, you can start to optimally lead and motivate them, but not a second earlier. Without that foundation of trust, your team will have a very hard time performing at a high level.

Now, this is not "conventional" management thinking, as you may have guessed. And this is a good thing. Being an effective Virtual Boss means doing things differently. Sometimes it means doing things in a very unconventional way. This calls for employing a leadership style that "average" bosses just don't use.

Here's a newsflash for you: "Average" bosses don't bother with trust at all. To optimally lead your staff and unleash the results you crave for your customers while pushing your direct reports to reach their potential, you need to get on the same page as your staff. You need to speak their language. And the only way they'll respond to you is if they implicitly trust you.

And the way to get them to trust you is to make regular deposits in the Trust Account, which is what this first section is all about.

MAKE REGULAR DEPOSITS IN THE TRUST ACCOUNT

Chances are that you have a bank account where your money is stored for safekeeping. Every week, you make regular deposits into, and withdrawals from, that bank account:

- Base salary, bonuses, expense checks, and other deposits increase the balance in that account.

- Cash withdrawals, debit card purchases, checks, living, and entertainment expenses decrease the balance.

Unless you enjoy bouncing checks and incurring overdraft fees, you're careful to monitor your balances. Even though you may have overdraft protection, you certainly don't want to pay that 16.75% overdraft penalty, so you're careful to make sure your deposits outweigh your withdrawals.

Similar to how you manage your bank accounts, each member of your staff has a virtual Trust Account that only you have the PIN for. In the same way that you make daily or weekly deposits into your real-world bank account, you make daily and weekly trust deposits in each of your people's virtual Trust Accounts.

To keep your staff highly motivated and productive, your goal is to make as many deposits in their Trust Accounts as you possibly can, and avoid making many, if any, withdrawals.

It goes without saying that your deposits should always outweigh your withdrawals. With Trust Accounts, you never want to be overdrawn, because there is no overdraft protection.

The more deposits you make, the more your people will produce superior results for themselves, the company, and you.

YOU MUST DO IT CONSTANTLY

For the average Virtual Boss, establishing trust with their people is not something they ever think about.

The truth is that trust is the single most important element in any relationship—whether the relationship is a personal or a business one.

It's a simple formula:

- When your team trusts you, they produce for you.
- When your team REALLY trusts you, they REALLY produce for you.

And superior performance from your team is what you're after, right? Most bosses completely ignore this fact … but you won't.

If you start to make small deposits in the respective Trust Accounts of your team every day, you'll see your *leadership effectiveness* significantly increase. From there, a funny thing will start to happen. You'll notice that your *team's performance* significantly improves too.

IT MIGHT SEEM CORNY

Getting people to trust you seems like a corny thing to be talking about when all you really want to do is make more money, get promoted, and work less gruelling hours, right?

Corny? Yeah, maybe a little. Soft? Possibly. But you need to set those thoughts aside.

When it comes to virtual management:

Conventional thinking leads to
conventional results.

Do you want conventional (read: average) results? No way! You want more than that—you want UNCONVENTIONAL (read: wildly successful) results!

Unconventional thinking leads to
unconventional results.

When you start making deposits in your people's Trust Accounts you'll have taken the very first step in producing UNCONVENTIONAL results.

SO WHEN DO YOU START MAKING THESE TRUST ACCOUNT DEPOSITS ANYWAY?

This is an easy one to answer. If you haven't already started, then you've waited too long!

Here's the thing, all you need to do is start early and implement often. If you are re-establishing trust or establishing it for the first time, then start making deposits in that person's Trust Account as soon as you can.

In fact, start a precedent of trust right from the get-go, even before someone starts working for you!

How? Head to Chapter 1 to find out.

CHAPTER 1
When to start making
Trust Account deposits

FOUR PROVEN TECHNIQUES

It's very important to start your relationship with any new hire with a precedent of trust right from the get-go. We'll get into how to establish or even re-establish trust with your current team in the coming chapters. But in this chapter, we'll talk about how you can make Trust Account deposits before you even hire someone.

Here are four proven techniques to make unexpected deposits right from the start:

1. Set the base salary range slightly below where it normally is.

2. Use unexpected sign-on bonuses.

3. Use unexpected guarantees.

4. Over-deliver on base salary (if possible).

The important part of all these techniques is to "under-promise and over-deliver." Everyone likes a pleasant surprise to the upside. That "element of surprise" is at play here.

Let me ask you: Wouldn't you be positively psyched to work for a new boss if they got you MORE money than you were originally expecting? I know I would. And it happened to me in my second sales job where the hiring manager used some of the above techniques on me. The result was that I never worked harder for anyone in my life. I felt like I owed him because he went above and beyond what I ever expected he would do for me.

You want to create that same sensation with your new hires.

People don't expect this kind of treatment. That's why these techniques are so effective in creating trust right at the onset by making early and effective deposits in the Trust Account.

So here we go …

1. MAKE DEPOSITS RIGHT AT "SALARY TIME"

When hiring, make every effort to get the candidate a little bit more on the base salary than they may have been expecting. This goes a long way in making deposits in the Trust Account.

When speaking to the candidate initially, take the average base pay of your company and then knock off a few thousand dollars. You can set this expectation with the recruiter you use as well. Typically a few thousand dollars won't make much difference in the types of candidates you may attract, but this simple technique will go a long way in endearing trust and "making deposits" when someone new comes on board.

By setting the base salary slightly below where the company typically starts, the candidate's expectation has been set. When it comes time to negotiate base pay and hire them, this fact can now be leveraged to successfully make a Trust Account deposit.

For example, say your base pay package is between $45,000 and $55,000 (depending on experience, track record, and the like). When you first meet with your candidate, tell them the base pay package is between $45,000 and $50,000 (note the lower amount on the high end). Make it clear to them throughout the interview process that the base package is between $45,000 and $50,000 depending on experience.

When you finally identify your candidate and it's time to make the formal offer, if you offer them $55,000, the candidate will be stunned. Most importantly, you have immediately set the tone for your relationship with them. You have set a clear message to them that you are their advocate and will do what it takes to go to the wall for them. This will pay big dividends for you in the future.

When negotiating salary, another approach you may want to take is in saying:

> "I'm not sure if I can do this and I don't want to promise anything, but let me see what I can do."

When you come back and tell them that you got them $5,000 over the amount the company typically pays, this will have two magical effects:

1. The candidate will feel extremely important (more on this later).

2. The candidate will think: "they want me so bad they overpaid to get me to work for them, I must be pretty special."

It also makes them feel indebted to you, leaving them with a strong desire to produce for "the boss who got me a little extra." You are now the lucky recipient of an extremely thankful, indebted, and motivated staff member in an excellent position to produce superior results for you.

Some would say that this form of trust-building is deceptive. I disagree. After all, your job is to hire the right person and secure the right match for your opening.

By withholding the higher levels of base pay to the candidate, you are merely extending the interviewing process to help screen for the best candidate. If someone wants to work for you at $50,000/year, then they'll REALLY want to work for you at $55,000/year.

2. USE SIGN-ON BONUSES

If making exceptions to your company base pay ranges are more difficult to advocate for, another effective salary Trust Account technique can be used.

When you first meet with the candidate, share with them that the base salary is between $45,000 and $55,000 (as it is). However, in the background, do a little negotiating with your Human Resources department or boss ahead of time to set the stage. Make the case that when you have high performers with solid track records at the ready for hire, you can give some of those individuals a sign-on bonus of say, $5,000.

Your business case is that $5,000 will be a small one-time fee to pay and not a recurring cost to the company. This bonus helps the candidate get "over the hump" if they currently have a base above your salary range. If this is thrown in at the end of the salary negotiations, this little extra one-time bonus will have the same uplifting effects as Technique #1.

3. USE GUARANTEES

If one of the other salary scenarios is not possible and your company has some kind of bonus structure as a form of compensation, can you get your company to guarantee the candidate's first bonus payment or two? If the "ramp up" period is, say, six months on average, make the case to get them a two-quarter guarantee.

The most important part of all these techniques is to not let the candidate be aware of this at any time during the interviewing process. Make this a "bonus" for them at the very end. If it comes as a complete surprise, there is a very low likelihood that they'll refuse your offer.

4. OVER-DELIVER ON BASE SALARY

On the opposite end of the salary spectrum, if the candidate's current base is $35,000 and your company's range is $45,000 to $55,000, tell them the actual range up-front, but inform them that "salaries are calculated by HR based on experience and previous base salary."

When you make the offer, don't offer $45,000 no matter what. Everyone has a high opinion of themselves when it comes to self-worth. So in this case, tell them the range, but then make your offer between $46,000 and $47,000. Validate it to your boss and to HR that the extra thousand dollars on the base are negligible over the long haul.

Bringing someone on board "at the minimum" typically produces "at the minimum" results. Therefore, by paying a new team member higher than the minimum starting salary, "at the minimum" results are avoided.

If you get internal resistance, remind them that an extra $1,000 over 26 pay periods (or however frequently you are paid) is a mere $38.46/fortnight. You can state your case by saying: *"Wouldn't you agree that we can afford $38.46 a fortnight to get a high-quality highly motivated person on board?"* HR will have a hard time disagreeing with you.

Why do these salary techniques work in getting people motivated and immediately trusting you?

It works because of one of the most powerful laws of human nature, called the Law of Reciprocity, which is explained in the next chapter.

CHAPTER 1 TAKEAWAYS

» Get your new hires a little bit more than the base they are expecting.

» Use sign-on bonuses.

» Use guarantees.

» Over-deliver on base salary for new hires with lower salary ranges than what your company offers.

CHAPTER 2

Make Trust Account deposits part of your everyday routine

THE LAW OF RECIPROCITY

For our purposes, the Law of Reciprocity states:

> If you do something nice for someone, human nature compels the recipient to do something nice for you in return.

The most important part of this law to remember, however, is that reciprocity is IMPLICIT. Meaning you should never mention that you need something in return. When someone does something nice for you, they implicitly expect that when the circumstances are right, you will do something of approximately equal value for them.

In the case of our newly hired team members, if you go the extra mile for them on their base salary, the Law of

Reciprocity mandates that they will go the extra mile for you in return. Always remember that people do expect repayment over time and this is based on the idea of human social interchange.

LET THEM TAKE ALL THE CREDIT FOR THE GOOD STUFF

"It is amazing what you can accomplish if you do not care who gets the credit." —**HARRY TRUMAN**

Never take the credit for the good work of your people. Remember, at one point in your career, you were most likely a pretty good front-line employee and that's probably how you got promoted to management. Now, as a manager of others, the time for individual glory has passed.

Your role now is to look good by helping others get results for themselves. More pointedly, your number one job is to get results through others, not get direct results on your own. The glory for you comes as the proud boss who watches from the sidelines as your people do it on their own.

The better your people perform, and the more they do it on their own, the better you look. If you are a new boss, this is an especially difficult mindset to change because most top-performing people are driven primarily for and by themselves.

Have confidence in your own competence and ability to perform as a great Virtual Boss, either on your own or through what you learn via this book. Don't feel insecure or threatened by the work of your people, especially those that are better than you were when you were in their role.

Their success is your success.

Let them take all the glory. When you do, you'll put even more deposits in the Trust Account. In the end, your Trust Account balance will be overflowing. And remember, the biggest account balance wins because the boss with the biggest account balance has the most motivated team raring to produce big results.

NO ONE LIKES TO BE TOLD WHAT TO DO—SUGGEST INSTEAD

I've never known anyone that really enjoys being told what to do. People love to think they're in control, when at all possible. Obviously, this is not always realistic. In later chapters, we'll review how to get your team to do things without giving orders. However, there will be times that you'll have to tell your people in no uncertain terms what they need to do in a given situation.

How you say it is the most important part, however.

Ben Franklin, one of the greatest statesmen of the modern era, would always advocate that when at all possible, "avoid giving direct orders." Never dictate or decree. Whenever possible, request, imply or make suggestions instead.

EXAMPLES:

Instead of: "I want you to ..."

Go with: "It might be a good idea if you ..." or "If I were you I would ..." or "You may want to consider ..."

One of my favorites here is: "May I make a suggestion?"

After they say yes, then give your suggestion. This method is far more effective and less dictatorial than: "No, no, no, what you need to do is ..."

If they don't implement your suggestion, you can then take it up with them by saying: "I thought we agreed that you would do ..."

The key work in this sentence is "we."

By making a "we" decision, the staff member remembers the interaction as something you and they decided together, not just you as their boss.

The chances of consistent follow-up are that much greater now that they have taken ownership (a very important concept we'll discuss later).

Important caveat: The above strategy works extremely well, but not in an emergency situation. If the house is on fire, then don't stand around and ask questions like these. Take action and dictate when it's needed.

A CRAZY TWIST!

Chances are, your team hates it when you call them or request to "jump on a call."

Admit it, they dread the completely unsolicited "not-you-returning-their-phone-call" call from you. They hate it because it can only mean one thing for them: more work.

These phone calls typically begin with you saying something like: "*If you wouldn't mind, we have a really short timeline on this but I need you to get me ...*" before you then launch right into whatever it is you need them to do (no idle chit-chat whatsoever) and start demanding whatever information you need. I know you do it. We all do it. And we all do it too much.

Here's a crazy twist. Have you ever just gotten on a call with any of your people out of the clear blue and asked them if there's anything YOU can do for THEM?

Most of them would nearly die from shock. I'd be willing to bet they are so used to you calling them to tell them to do something, that their reaction will be positively priceless … in a good way.

So turn the tables and make some serious deposits in their Trust Account in the process. The first time you do it, they'll be so flabbergasted they probably won't know what to say.

That'll be a good indication that you should probably keep doing it on a semi-regular basis.

Remember that one of the most important parts of the Trust Account is reinforcing the idea that both you and they WANT EXACTLY THE SAME THING. Namely, you want them to be as successful as they can possibly be.

Remember, if they are successful, you are successful. It's just that simple.

So here's how the "how can I help you" phone call would go:

You: "Hello Sandi, this is Ralph."

Sandi (staff member): "Oh hi Ralph, what's going on?"

You: "Nothing much, I had a few minutes and I just wanted to call to see if you needed help with anything?"

Sandi: (obviously in a state of shock) "… uh, well, I don't think so, but well actually, there is something I'd like to discuss with you …"

Make even more consistent deposits in their Trust Account by surprising your people today with the unsolicited "how can I help you" call. You'll end up "shocking" them into superior job performance.

When I was first writing this chapter, it prompted me to do exactly the above with one of my people. (I have to admit, I hadn't done something like that in a while.) A day or so later, she called me and told me: "I have NEVER had a boss EVER call me just out of the blue and ask me if he could help me. I am so happy you are my boss."

That week, she closed three new customer accounts worth a total of $1.2 million. I kid you not.

Did the "how can I help you call" do it? Probably not. But it didn't hurt.

IF YOU SCREW UP, JUST ADMIT IT

"More people would learn from their mistakes if they weren't so busy denying them." —HAROLD J SMITH

Do you have a difficult time admitting you have made a mistake?

You shouldn't. Because the thing is, you actually build credibility by admitting you've made a mistake.

I know it's not easy to admit, but as a boss who has stuff thrown at you all the time, with the constant pressure to perform, I have news for you: you're not going to get everything right all the time.

If you screw up, just admit it. It's OK not to be perfect.

In fact, your people will notice this and respect you even more because of it. It makes you more REAL. And they'll like you and respect you even more because of it.

As a leader, you may push and drive your team to be perfect, but none of them will be perfect either. Perfection is a great goal to shoot for, but in reality, it's completely unattainable. That's because humans are, by nature, imperfect creatures with many faults.

Here's the bottom line: When you make a mistake, admit it. You'll deepen your level of trust with your staff when you do because they'll see a little of themselves in you. They'll realize that you are a little bit more like them than maybe you care to admit.

You'll become "transparent." And being transparent is a very good thing.

Plus, from their perspective, who really wants to work for Mr. or Mrs. Perfect?

It's important, however, to beware of making the same mistakes over and over, and admitting them over and over. If you do that, your team will think you're just plain incompetent.

You also need to be careful of taking this tip too far and making a big deal about admitting your mistakes and/or doing it too frequently in an attempt to build trust quickly. Your team may perceive this humbleness as insincere and you want to seem real and transparent to them, not disingenuous.

Admit your mistakes subtly, without fanfare, and strengthen the bond you have with your staff while making hefty deposits in their Trust Account in the process.

GET ON A CALL, DAMMIT!

In a study from 2018, it was discovered that the average worker spends 28 percent of their work week on email. This is more than 11 hours a week! With the average person sending and receiving 124 work emails every day, or 620 emails every week, we're spending an average of 1.1 minutes on each email.

With the portability and ease of email, it's no wonder this is the case. It's just so darn easy to anonymously pound out an email instead of dealing with the realities of actually TALKING to people about some uncomfortable or complex issue.

It's so safe, it's so convenient and it's so, so ... ineffective.

Establishing trust, however, is a hard thing to do when the main way you communicate with your team is via email or even through a tool like Slack. As an ambitious Virtual Boss, it's critical for you to establish (or re-establish) actual human contact with your staff—and you can't do this by email no matter how "human" you make it.

To lead effectively, you need to "get in their grill"; talk to them on an actual call, understand their views, consider their solutions, then work together to take the right course of action.

To let you off the hook, you are probably responding to the majority of your emails either after normal working hours or squeezing them in between meetings or calls when you have a little time. In these cases, email is very handy.

But I'm sure there are plenty of times when you respond or initiate an email chain when you KNOW you should probably call. In those cases, pick up the phone or send them a Zoom link. Reinforce your people's trust in you by talking to them. Don't manage them from behind the façade of email.

BE PRESENT

No one likes to feel like they are playing second fiddle.

As you know, there are multiple distractions when you are working with your staff. There are text messages, emails, Slack IMs, phone calls, and Zoom call interruptions— all vying for your time at any given moment. No doubt, there's always a lot going on (you are very busy after all).

So you answer all those incoming calls and you get on all those conference calls ... while you ignore your staff members. You may think you're doing the right thing. "I'm multitasking," you say. You aren't. You're making Trust Account *withdrawals*.

In fact, every time you text, email, take an incoming call or are distracted in any way when you should be spending quality time with your team, you're unwittingly making small withdrawals from the Trust Account, perhaps without even realizing it.

Your team notices you not paying attention to them, and although they tell you "don't worry about it," they don't like it. So do yourself a big favor, push all those distractions aside and be present. Even if it's on a Zoom call, *be present*—be available and attentive. If you're never really "with them" when you're with them, you'll never really know what's going on in their world.

You need to be vigilant about establishing, then maintaining good old human contact with them—which is far harder to do in a virtual management world but it *can* be done.

And when you establish good old human contact, you reinforce trust. Because when you're with your team, paying undivided attention to them, and being present, it's the best present you can give to both them and you.

YOUR TIME FOR INDIVIDUAL GLORY HAS PASSED

Do you frequently walk down memory lane with your team?

Let's admit it; you were most likely a very good staff member before you became a Virtual Boss. In fact, you were so good, you were probably recognized by your boss and were promoted to the position you're in now.

Do you find yourself starting lots of conversations with your team with: "Well when I was doing your job …"? The problem is that your team doesn't care about how great you were.

Here's a newsflash for you:

Your team only cares about how great THEY perform.

Every time you remind them of your past brilliance, you unwittingly make small withdrawals from the Trust Account, whittling away that trust currency you have worked so hard to accumulate over time.

When you talk about your past achievements, you make two big mistakes:

1. You underscore the separation between them and you by subtly reminding them that you are management and they are front-line staff members. This misalignment creates resentment over time if you're not careful.

2. You pull the spotlight away from them; thereby minimizing their importance in a roundabout way.

A better idea is to bite your tongue when you want to launch into one of your "when I was doing your job …" diatribes. Instead, place the staff members on a pedestal and force yourself to stay firmly on the ground.

After all, your time for individual glory has passed. Your team are the stars now.

THE POPULARITY CONTEST IS OVER

Did all the girls love you in high school? Or did all the boys want to ask you out? Were you deluged with dates for your Senior Prom? Were you always invited to the best parties?

I wasn't. I couldn't quite figure out where I fit in high school.

Was I a jock? Was I a nerd? Or was I just a jazz band geek? All I knew was that I wasn't super popular, but I really wanted to be.

Do you have this same desire now as a boss?

The working world is not a popularity contest like it was in high school. The best high-performing Virtual Bosses don't end up dating the head cheerleader and don't get invited to the Senior Prom by the starting quarterback.

Sometimes, being a great boss requires you to be *unpopular* with your team. It requires you to make tough decisions that sometimes, even though they may be in the best interests of your team, are very unpopular. It's a fine line between wanting to be liked by your team and establishing trust. Making deposits in the Trust Account is all about consistently doing the RIGHT things and not about doing popular things.

Here's the thing:

- Sometimes, establishing trust means holding firm on the company line.
- Other times it means you lead your team in the exact opposite direction.

- Sometimes it means being rigorous and tough.
- Other times it means being thoughtful and understanding.

Whatever the situation, ask yourself:

"Am I leading my team this way because it's the popular thing to do or because it's the right thing to do?"

If you come to the conclusion that it's only the popular thing to do, then rethink your actions. In the end, you may not be loved by your team, but you will be respected. And if you can establish trust and respect, you're on your way to unleashing the very best from them.

So the next time you're faced with making a tough decision, do the right thing, not the popular thing.

"GIRL EARS"

I recall a story I heard about a CEO who was having a conversation with his 10-year-old daughter. He was scrolling through his iPhone as he listened to her speak. She soon realized that she didn't have her father's complete attention.

"Dad," she said. "I want you to listen with girl ears."

As a boss, I'm sure you're guilty of it just like I am—too

much multitasking! We read our emails while we listen to our voicemails, tap on our laptop as we speak with our people, talk on our cell phones while paying for the groceries, and on and on. We all think that we are making the most efficient use of our time. But are we?

In actuality, how much information do we all fail to process when we're not really paying attention to either of the two activities we are trying to perform simultaneously?

If you're too busy to devote your full attention to your team, they will get the feeling that you just don't care. You may be making withdrawals from the Trust Account without even realizing it. And as a top-performing Virtual Boss, you don't want this. Because a person who feels valued is a person who feels good about themselves.

And a person who feels good about themselves produces better, higher quality results. After all, isn't this what you want?

THE "SEAGULL MANAGER"

Have you ever worked for a "Seagull Manager"?

It's the kind who seldom interacts with his people but occasionally swoops down, dumps on everybody, and then quickly flies away. If you haven't guessed already, this is not exactly the kind of leadership we advocate here.

When you're all stressed out, productivity is plummeting and your boss just called you for the fifth time today to yell at you, do you become a seagull? Granted, it's hard to keep your emotions in check and think clearly at times like these.

Instead, look at it as an opportunity. It's in times like these when you need to rise above the pressures, and show your true mettle as a manager and make big deposits in the Trust Account in the process. Your team knows you're under pressure, so now is not the time to come down on them. Now is the time to ELEVATE your people, not dump on them. Because this is when they need you most.

Anyone can manage a team when times are good. But the top managers are at their BEST when times are WORST. This is the crucible of leadership and management. So I challenge you to establish trust instead.

Go ahead, make those Trust Account deposits—and do it by making a connection. Connection only occurs when there is an environment that promotes active two-way interaction. To build connections and gain understanding, top-performing managers need to come out from behind their desks and embrace a "get in your grill" passion for interaction.

Tom Peters called it "Management by Wandering Around" or MBWA. I call it "Management by Virtually Wandering Around" or MBVWA.

So get out in the environment of your team, let them see you. Get into your Slack threads and your Project Management task threads. Make the connection so memorable it will not be forgotten. Comment, share, praise, prod. If your people are reluctant to interact, that's OK, keep doing it anyway. Demonstrate your commitment to making the connection through two-way interaction. All the while you're making more deposits in that ol' Trust Account.

And whatever you do, stay away from the seagulls.

"GIRL SCOUT POWER"

I once read a story about Frances Hesselbein. Just recently named as president of the Girl Scouts of America, she knew the organization was teetering on the edge of extinction.

The Girl Scouts, an organization of thousands of volunteers from across the fifty states, had been going about their business in a very traditional way for years.

But that way was now placing the organization in jeopardy.

How could she motivate a group of thousands of volunteers?

Because her position had no inherent power to command, she quickly realized that she couldn't ORDER the necessary changes in behavior. She understood that by INCLUDING as many people as possible in the process of change, she could harness the power of others to achieve the important goals she was responsible for achieving.

Although we cover this concept in far greater detail in further chapters, this is precisely what the top-performing Virtual Boss does. The top-performing Virtual Boss follows this creed.

"The more power you GIVE, the more you GET."

As a boss, do you wield power or do you give it away like Frances Hesselbein?

It's tough. There's so much coming at you every day, it's difficult not to lapse into an "I order—you do" kind of management style. In spite of that, top-performing bosses rise above the fray and do not succumb to the temptation to command.

Instead of commanding, they unleash the best from their team by GIVING AWAY their power, so that their team BECOMES empowered.

So put one of your people in charge of a big project, allow them to show their brilliance and empower them to do it to the best of their ability. We'll get into this even more in subsequent chapters, but the idea is to let your people feel empowered to make decisions by placing them in charge and letting them get to work. It will keep them highly engaged, motivated and at a very high-performance level.

BE "AUTHENTIC"

"The true test of a man's character is what he does when no one is watching." —JOHN WOODEN

Being authentic simply means being yourself. If you are a new boss or maybe one that has struggled in the past and is trying to behave differently towards your people in the interest of getting better results from them, don't stray from who you are.

Just because your boss may be an autocrat, doesn't mean that you should be one. If one of your colleagues is a soft touch, it doesn't mean that you should be that way either.

The best thing to do is to take elements of all the great bosses and incorporate them into your style. Use these elements to craft your own style of management. Remember that the leadership style that works the best is the one that feels right to you.

The most important part of this is that regardless of style, always be genuine. Because if you're not genuine, your people will know. They are far more observant and perceptive than you may give them credit for. They will know when you're not being you.

So be yourself, stick to your style, incorporate the learnings from this chapter and you'll be on the right path.

SO, NOW WHAT?

A common theme in this book is to always be aware that your people are way smarter than you may think they are. This is not to say you think they're dumb, of course not.

What this means is that your team picks up on your subtle moves, moods and messages far more than you are aware that they do. They notice things, and they're watching your every move. And what they notice most is your authenticity.

Are you authentic when you deliver a message to them? Or are you manipulating them so that you can achieve your own agenda?

They are constantly gauging if your words match your actions. They are always monitoring to see if you do what you say and say what you do. If you say you want them to trust you, are you doing the small things every day that will make it easy for them to trust you?

When you start to make deposits in the Trust Account, you must be genuine.

If you start using the techniques in this chapter and begin to work them into your everyday leadership activities, but you come across as insincere, the techniques simply will not work.

In fact, they may actually have the opposite effect.

A lot of this hinges on how you feel about the team that works for you. (This will be a discussion in later chapters.)

The bottom line is this: the superior boss's words match their actions.

What this means is that if you say that you will call at a certain time, you call at that time. If you say you will do X, Y and Z, you do X, Y and Z.

So don't delay, start making deposits in the Trust Account starting now.

CHAPTER 2 TAKEAWAYS

» Evoke the Law of Reciprocity.

» Let your employees take all the credit for the good stuff.

» Suggest instead of command.

» Call your employees and ask them what YOU can do for THEM.

» If you screw up, admit it.

» With uncomfortable or complex issues, make a call instead of hiding behind an email.

» When you are working with your employees one-on-one, be present.

» When coaching your employees, don't ever start a statement with "When I was doing your job ..."

» Focus on making the right decision, not the popular decision.

» When interacting with your employees, focus on them ONLY and do not multitask.

» Do not be a "Seagull Manager": when times are tough, be an eagle and assess what needs to be done, block out the noise and get out from behind the desk and Manage By Virtually Wandering Around (MBVWA).

» Empower your employees.

» ALWAYS be authentic.

CHAPTER 3

Make Trust Account deposits when dealing with corporate insanity

BE THE "POP-UP BLOCKER"

This is not news to you, but there's a high likelihood that there is a lot of B.S. that gets hurled at you every day. Be it through emails or Slack messages; initiatives of all kinds come at you and your team all the time.

One of your many jobs is to shield your people from this BS as much as possible by both screening what you redirect to them and by which initiatives you support.

Think of yourself as your people's "pop-up blocker"— shielding them from irrelevant "pop-ups" while making sure they focus their time and attention on working.

For those "pop-up" initiatives that you feel add little worth, do all you can to advocate these initiatives with the bare minimum of effort, while simultaneously meeting the corporate objectives. Bear in mind that with this approach, many initiatives may never make it to your people because of your filtering. This is OK. Your main job, after all, is to help them produce excellent results for customers. The interesting part of this concept is that when they uncover that you filter initiatives on their behalf, the more indebted to you they'll become.

When filtering what reaches them, you send a subtle yet effective message to them that you are doing all you can to create an environment with an unremitting focus on working. They will realize that you, as their boss, are immune to getting caught up in the multiple programs that satisfy some upper-level executive's ego because of some concept he learned at Harvard Business School.

Nevertheless, if there is a new initiative that could potentially help them to produce more effectively, then become an advocate for that initiative in spades. By being selective about which programs you fully support, your people will faithfully follow your lead on the important ones, while minimizing the impact from the not-so-important ones.

Become exceedingly discriminating as to which corporate ventures you support and always be mindful of what's in it for your people. Your selectivity as to which ones you are standing behind will be noticed.

When the program can potentially help them to either be more successful or make them more money, and you have established a pattern of selectivity in your advocacy for different programs, then when you finally do endorse a program with vigor, your people will fall in line behind you in your advocacy.

POKE FUN AT THE COMPANY

It may seem like an irreverent thing to do, but lightly poking fun at the "corporate ridiculousness" endears you to your people. It earns you credibility and it allows them to see you as real—and not as some corporate stooge.

All companies have them: The initiatives that make no sense whatsoever, the contests that demotivate instead of motivate, the endless administrative work that actually impairs your people's ability to be effective at their jobs. When you poke fun at these things, it keeps you real and transparent, someone your team can identify with.

In fact, the more bureaucracy that exists in your organization, the more opportunity there is to gently poke fun at the company while keeping your mission, as well as the mission of the organization, foremost. The key is that once you rake the organization over the coals, you must immediately get them back on track and explain the "why" from the corporate perspective. Keep it real. Get them back on board with the mission, while sifting through the bureaucracy.

If you get an overwhelming amount of resistance to any particular policy, make sure you frame it in reality. Unless you're at a start-up company, chances are that the company you work for will have some standard operating procedures that make little, if any sense. If you cannot change the policy (worth a try), then you can always make fun of it, then get your team all back on track so the frustration doesn't reach out of control levels.

What if your people still don't get it? Then you may need to give them a little dose of reality. Tell them:

> "The only place where you can make all the decisions and assure yourselves that they are all sensible is if you run the show."

That's right, if they run the business, they can then make the rules. Remind them that running your own business has an incredibly long list of "cons" that outweigh that "pro" as well.

Rest assured, all companies have "corporate ridiculousness"—it's part of the trade-off of working for someone else. Dealing with bureaucracy and idiotic corporate initiatives is part of the contract you sign on for when you work for someone else, so deal with it as best as you can. It will be just the same somewhere else as well, if not worse.

Telling them this serves two important purposes:

1. It gives them a quick "reality check." (We all need them sometimes.)

2. It improves your team's retention. (If they are getting "fed up with it all," you can gently remind them that the grass is NOT always greener somewhere else.)

CHAPTER 3 TAKEAWAYS

» Filter the BS and be a pop-up blocker for your employees.

» It is OK to gently poke fun at the company, but make sure to explain the "why" from a corporate perspective.

CHAPTER 4

Make Trust Account deposits when your people mess up

ALWAYS GET THEIR SIDE OF THE STORY

It may seem obvious, but when there is an issue involving one of your team, ALWAYS get your rep's side of the story before passing judgment. Sounds simple to do, but in practice, it's very difficult, especially when hundreds of different things are coming at you every day.

I am amazed by how many Virtual Bosses miss this opportunity to be fair and at the same time pass up a golden opportunity to make a huge Trust Account deposit. Part of the problem is that doing this correctly takes time, and time is not something a boss has very much of.

When something adverse happens to one of your team, force yourself to call the person (or get on a Zoom if needed) to get their side of the story first. NOTHING will go further in helping you make further deposits in the Trust Account. Even when the pressure is to act quickly and berate, pause and contact the person to hear their side first—it makes all the difference.

As the saying goes:

> "There are three sides to every story: yours, theirs and the truth."

Keep this quote in mind the next time you hear of one of your people making some huge mistake or screw up.

No matter how bad it seems or how guilty your staff member may appear, in 99.9% of cases, how events unfolded as told by someone else is not what actually happened. You need to get their side first. When you call the person, approach it like this:

> "I may not have all the details correct, but I have been told that you did (the bad thing that happened). I'm sure there is more to the story, so please tell me what happened."

Here's a personal anecdote from my sales manager years:

A few years back, I had an incident where one of my salespeople was distributing pricing materials that were not fully approved by corporate. Somehow, our VP of Sales found out about it. At 4:45 pm on a Friday afternoon, the VP of Sales called me demanding to know what the hell our salesperson was doing as this was grounds for firing. He demanded that I address the issue immediately, and if I did not I would be in serious trouble as well.

I could feel a wave of sickness coming over me as he described the consequences.

As anyone would do in a case like this, I immediately called her—fully intending to vent my frustration and threaten her with firing if she didn't have a good explanation.

Somehow, better judgment prevailed and I quickly hung up before she could answer.

I then took a deep breath and asked myself why she would do something like this. Seeing how she was my singular best rep, if I knew her well, she most likely had a pretty good reason. After all, she had never done anything like this previously. In fact, she had a superb track record of both sales and behavior.

After that momentary pause, I got her on the phone. Doing my best to control my emotions, I asked her calmly:

> "I may not have all the details correct, but I have been told that you have been using inappropriate pricing materials in several accounts. I am sure that there is more to the story, so please tell me what happened."

I found out she had been working feverishly to disseminate the correct pricing materials, but had inadvertently made a typographical error that she had not noticed. To get new pricing brochures would have taken two weeks to be delivered. In her haste, she had printed out copies from her computer, put together the week before. The pricing brochure contained a severe disparity that she had not noticed.

I calmly asked her how many offices she had dropped the information off to. She responded that it was about fifteen offices. I told her to go to each office on Monday, retrieve the brochures, destroy them and never use them again.

I also asked her to write an email explaining how she would be rectifying her mistake and to send it to me, my boss and the VP of Sales. This was her only hope to not get fired.

She did all the above and was never fired.

I never had another incident like that with her. She had learned her lesson that no matter the urgency, don't cut corners.

If I had given in to my original urge, (and who would have blamed me) no one would have benefited. We all would have lost. Instead, she and I created a proactive plan to rectify the situation. And because we did this together; it never turned into a "you versus me" confrontation.

If at all possible, take the fall for your people publicly. Never hang them out to dry in public. And always reprimand in private.

The best part is that she ended that year ranked in the #1 team in the country, winning our President's Club Award. I am not making this up. Additionally, based on her prodigious skills, she was promoted to the home office the following year. Just imagine if I had ripped into her? I was so close to doing it.

Please remember this lesson the next time this kind of situation happens to you.

PROTECT THEM

"He can't do that to our pledges … Only we can do that to our pledges."—OTTER AND BOON, ANIMAL HOUSE

When the situation warrants, take responsibility for your people's mistakes publicly. If you don't have all the facts as to what exactly happened, hold back from making a judgment until you have all the facts. Remember, only you are allowed to criticize your people. No one else is, not even your boss.

If you let others get away with it, then you'll be on a runaway freight train you'll never gain control of. The bottom line is that you should never let anyone say anything negative about your people in a public forum and let them get away with it. If you adhere to this principle always, you'll develop a reputation as a strong leader and advocate for your people, even when the chips are down.

Anyone can be a great leader when things are going well. When you and your people are under fire is when you can really show your mettle as a leader. By publicly sticking up for your people, you'll further strengthen your trust with them, while making hefty deposits in the Trust Account.

NEVER BERATE YOUR TEAM—AND MOST IMPORTANTLY, NEVER DO IT IN PUBLIC

The best scenario is to never berate your people, either publicly or privately. But if someone (your boss, a co-worker, or any other operational personnel) says anything publicly about your staff members that is less than flattering, vigorously defend them, even if your people are seemingly in the wrong. Once you understand their viewpoint, then you can decide what corrective action should be taken.

It's your job to "block" for them at times so that you get their side of the story and first understand their seemingly bewildering behavior.

Think of your role as that of the left tackle on a football team—the guy whose sole job it is to protect the quarterback's blind side from the oncoming snarling 240-pound blitzing defensive end. That would make you the left tackle and yes, your staff members the star quarterback. I know this is tough to admit, but it's true!

Protect them as much as you can and whatever you do, never hang them out to dry in public. Instead, get their side first, then if a reprimand is necessary, reprimand in private, always.

INNOCENT UNTIL PROVEN GUILTY

"Trust men and they will be true to you; treat them greatly and they will show themselves great."—RALPH WALDO EMERSON

Trust people until they give you a reason not to.

Do you trust your people to be conscientious, to tell the truth, do what's right, use common sense and work eight hours a day? You'd better. Don't hire someone unless you can trust them. The average Virtual Boss trusts their people only after they have proven that they are worthy of that trust. The "guilty until proven innocent" mentality is the biggest single destructor to a boss's ability to make things happen.

Don't give in to it, do the opposite—trust people first.

Don't wait for them to *earn* your trust because ... how smug is that?

Why would they feel like they should earn your trust? Yes, you are the boss, but who do you think you are?

Let's remember one basic thing: Most people are conscientious and honest, driven by a desire to do their jobs well. If you truly feel that all people are essentially bad and untrustworthy, then sorry to say, you may want to re-evaluate your career choice as a manager of people.

Being in a supervisory role demands that you possess a basic trust in people and possess a fundamental belief that humans are basically good at the core. If you think all people are untrustworthy and you're a boss, then your beliefs are in direct conflict with how best to do your job. The internal divergence of knowing that you need to trust people but never being able to actually do it will eat away at you constantly and turn an uncomfortable job into an unmanageable one.

Remember the Law of Reciprocity. It works for good things, but it also works in reverse.

"You reap what you sow" works when you show an inherent distrust for people. If you distrust your people, they'll sense it and they will distrust you. You cannot hide it. The truth will come out in your actions and your words.

Go out of your way to do nice and meaningful things for them. Remember that the great Virtual Boss is always looking for opportunities to make deposits in his team's Trust Accounts.

WHY TRUST ANYWAY?

As a wise man once said:

> "Trust is the glue that binds people together in groups."

When you are candid, open, consistent and predictable, there will be trust ... it's a logical consequence of honesty and truth-telling. That's all well and good you might say, but what does all this really do for you? I'll tell you. It allows your team to act so that the rules of the game aren't constantly changing.

This gives them peace of mind.

When they have peace of mind, then and only then, will they be willing to make the extra effort and place themselves on the line for both themselves and you. No person can produce superior performance if they don't do those things on a regular basis.

So make deposits in the Trust Account for what it gets both of you. And what it gets you is a person who always feels supported and comfortable in putting forth maximum effort. Those people will "go to the wall" for you.

And only when these things happen can stellar job performance be achieved. Work daily to establish trust, place those deposits in the Trust Account so your account is OVERFLOWING.

By the way, subsequent chapters in this book won't work unless you have established this critical first step.

One last thing on trust—yet another old expression:

"If you tell the truth you never have to remember what you said."

Who has time to remember more than they need to remember? At its base level, being trustworthy is far easier and far less stressful than the alternative approach. The key is this: always treat your staff as the END unto themselves.

What I mean is this: If your team gets a whiff of you using them to get YOU what YOU want, then you're sunk. You'll have a potential mutiny on your hands. Or worse yet, they'll just tune you out.

Nobody likes feeling used. I know I don't. Like you, I've been used by bosses before and it's the biggest demotivator I can think of.

Great bosses, however, NEVER use their team. They NEVER treat their people as a means to which they can achieve their own ends.

As we discussed before, if your team feels you have their back and they feel they can trust you, then you've laid the perfect foundation on which they can build their superior job performance empire.

The simple truth is this, trust is:

- Hard to earn
- Easy to lose
- When lost, nearly impossible to regain

So don't screw up all you've built by making stupid mistakes that you could have easily avoided!

Start implementing at least SOME of the material we've discussed so far. Do it tomorrow at the latest. Otherwise, it'll be really hard for you to take both your leadership and your team's job performance to the next level. So, don't delay. Take out your ATM card and head to the bank.

Because big Trust Account deposits lead to even bigger REAL bank deposits.

CHAPTER 4 TAKEAWAYS

» Always get your employees' side of the story before passing judgment.

» Stick up for your people; you are the only one who is allowed to criticize them.

» Never berate your employees—and most importantly, never do it in public.

» Your employees are innocent until proven guilty, NOT the other way around.

» NEVER use your employees.

ACTION GUIDE

SUGGEST INSTEAD OF DICTATE

Practice suggesting what to do instead of dictating it. As we learned, no one likes to be told what to do. To jog your memory, look back at Chapter 2 for some examples.

Think of a scenario in which you will have to imply or make suggestions to your team in the near future. Write out some examples of requests that you can make to your people to get your message across below.

_____

_____

_____

_____

_____

_____

_____

_____

_____

_____

_____

THE CRAZY TWIST

Write out a brief plan below of how and when you can do the "crazy twist": call up each of your team and ask them what you can do for them.

Also, think about how often you want to do this and put a reminder in your phone to ensure it gets done on a somewhat regular basis.

_____

_____

_____

_____

_____

_____

_____

_____

_____

_____

_____

_____

PICK UP THE PHONE!

Instead of emailing, practice getting comfortable with picking up the phone or getting on a Zoom call when a situation warrants.

There is probably a situation right now that may warrant a phone call, a group call with one of your execs, your boss or a friend. Instead of emailing or texting, FORCE yourself to pick up the phone and call to address the situation head-on. Think about what you are going to say and write it out below.

_____

_____

_____

_____

_____

_____

_____

_____

_____

_____

GIVE AWAY POWER

Write out three specific examples below on how you can give away power as you manage like Frances Hesselbein.

1. _____

_____

_____

_____

2. _____

_____

_____

_____

3. _____

_____

_____

_____

INNOCENT UNTIL PROVEN GUILTY

Regarding always hearing your team's side of the story before passing judgment, do you have an example like mine in Chapter 4, when you either handled it like I did before I thought twice or after I thought twice?

Perhaps you did the right thing. Perhaps you did not. How did your response make you feel? How did it make the person feel? What has been the effect of the incident on you and your staff members in the long run? If you had to do it all over again, how would you change what you did?

_____

_____

_____

_____

_____

_____

_____

_____

_____

REPORT CARD

EXERCISE 1

Over the next month, do a self-report card of how present you are for your team. Keep this book handy, and write out the names of your team.

At the end of your day working with them, think about how many phone calls, emails, texts, conference calls, calls from your boss you did while you were also interacting with your team. (For example, while you were in a Zoom meeting with them, were you also texting a friend or checking your emails?) Give yourself a little wiggle room because as we know, some interruptions are completely unavoidable. Be honest about the ones you know were avoidable and could have waited. Give yourself a grade as to how present you were with them during that filed interaction.

TEAM MEMBER NAME: _____

Notes: _____

_____

_____

_____

_____

Grade: _____

TEAM MEMBER NAME: _____

Notes: _____

_____

_____

_____

Grade: _____

TEAM MEMBER NAME: _____

Notes: _____

_____

_____

_____

Grade: _____

TEAM MEMBER NAME: _____

Notes: _____

_____

_____

_____

Grade: _____

EXERCISE 2

Give yourself a rating as to how good you have been with making the right decision versus the popular decision.

Think about a recent example of how you made the popular decision when you know the right decision would have made you less popular. Write out below what that incident was and how you would handle it differently in the future.

Incident:

1. _____

2. _____

3. _____

4. _____

5. _____

How I would handle it differently:

1. _____

2. _____

3. _____

4. _____

5. _____

EXERCISE 3

Over the next month, remain vigilant about decisions that you recognize as being ones where the right decision might not make you so popular. Then do the following:

Write out those incidents below and then give a brief description of how you plan to or did handle it.

Then be honest and rank yourself on how well you did on making the right decision.

INCIDENT	RANK

EXERCISE 4

Rank yourself as a "pop-up blocker."

Based on initiatives handed down to you in the last month, or over the next month, rank yourself on your ability to filter. If you give yourself anything but an A+, how can you improve on keeping your team from getting bogged down in anything but programs that will help them produce stellar job performance?

INITIATIVE	RANK

SECTION 1 - FINAL REFLECTION

Based on the previous exercises and what you've learned in this section, what do you need to improve on to be a better Virtual Boss?

_____

_____

_____

_____

_____

_____

_____

_____

_____

SECTION 2

THE SECRETS OF SETTING
THE BAR HIGHER

THE SECRETS OF SETTING THE BAR HIGHER

Don't you just love corporate buzzwords?

Some of my personal favorites:

"We need to start thinking outside the box."

"Let's take a deeper dive on that ..."

"We need to give it 110 percent!"

"Let's create a win-win for the customer."

"It's all about change management."

"Let's take that offline."

"At the end of the day ..."

"Let's produce some strong organic growth."

And my personal favorite:

"We need to set the bar high."

Here's the problem though: *everyone* is trying to "set the bar high."

And if everyone is "setting the bar high," does that mean that you should?

No way.

One of the pivotal themes throughout this book is to *not* do the things that everyone else is doing. Superior job performance comes from doing things *differently;* from being *unconventional* when everyone else is being *conventional.* Whatever you do, don't go along with the crowd, just because "everyone else is doing it."

If you do what "everyone else is doing" then as a Virtual Boss, you'll get precisely what everyone else is getting. Namely: Average, mediocre, conventional results for customers. And I doubt you would be reading this book right now if that's what you were really after.

So with all due respect to those who have ever used the "set the bar high" buzzword in explaining the direction of their team (myself included), this section is for you.

As you'll see, this book is all about continually challenging your team to reach higher than they think that they are capable of achieving. And because of the overuse of all the aforementioned "sales buzzwords" watering down the actual meaning of all these expressions, the expression "set the bar high," no longer has the punch it once did.

In this hyper-achieving world of getting top results in shorter periods of time, with information flying at you at light speed at all hours of the day and night, and corporate objectives becoming increasingly more and more aggressive, as a top-performing Virtual Boss, YOU need to buck the trend.

What you really need to do is to "set the bar high**er**" (notice the little "er" on the end of "high"). And by doing things differently, you'll have a base formula to produce superior results while separating yourself from your competition, your peers and those nasty corporate sales buzzwords. Now let's get into it.

CHAPTER 5

Be "The Measuring Stick"

Whether you like it or not, your staff members look to you as the measuring stick. As the boss, you are the one who sets the tone of the team. Your actions and discussions with them reflect your ideals, your tone, your style and most importantly, your expectations.

In the end, your team is a direct reflection of you. When you are talking about job performance, you need to make your expectations clear from the start and set the bar not just high, but higher.

In doing so, you are making a powerful statement of performance to them, and you make your team a direct reflection of your values, ideals and standards, and not those of the company.

WHAT DOES IT MEAN TO SET THE BAR *HIGHER?*

It means that your expectations of your team members are higher than both the expectations they have for themselves as well as the expectations the company has for them.

Be very clear about this right from the start. In fact, you should always underscore this fact whenever you interact with your people.

Let me say it again:

> *The expectations you have for them are higher than those that both the company sets for them and what they set for themselves.*

This sends a powerful message right from the start. **You will not tolerate mediocrity** in any of its forms.

Reinforce this point whenever and as frequently as you can. Shout it from the rooftops, if you can. Tap it out on emails; verbalize in your conversations with them, text it to them on their cell phones. Get the message out any way and as frequently as you can by saying things like:

- *"I hired you because you were someone who would never accept mediocrity."*

- *"Merely doing your job is being average! Do you aspire to be average?"*

- *"I didn't come here to finish (middle of the pack) and neither should you."*

Set the bar **higher** than the company.

Set the bar **higher** than your virtual management colleagues.

Set the bar **higher** than your boss.

The bar is set with the company goals and that's all well and good, however, your bar is set higher. Make the message very clear from the start—in your team, things are different. On your team, your goals are set higher than the company. Repeat it thousands of times in different ways.

It doesn't matter how you tell them, just tell them.

Yell it at them if you're a yeller …

Whisper it to them if you're a soft talker …

Joke with them about it if you're a joker …

Calmly discuss it with them if you are calm and cool …

Whatever you do, just do it … but *do it in your own way.*

Also, do it with little fanfare. Just make it as obvious to them as the sky is blue. They'll get the message.

RIGOROUS, NOT RUTHLESS

This standard is rigorous, yes, but is it ruthless? I think not.

What you are doing is creating a culture of discipline—a key trait of all extremely high-performing organizations. What you'll find is that the staff members that cannot take it will try to find a way at first to shy away, but in time, they'll find employment elsewhere (or maybe you will help them, as outlined later in this book).

THE "DICTATORSHIP"

Sometimes, the forcible approach is best. This is not a message that can be manipulated, debated, open for discussion or democratized. This is the edict you are dictating to them. Shoot for the stars and set the bar higher. Period. There is no other desired outcome.

In many ways and under many other circumstances, your team is a modified democracy. You want to empower your team; you want to allow them the autonomy to feel like they are making their own decisions on most things. Your open and flexible leadership tone makes them feel good about what they're doing and they feel like they have a measure of control over their destiny.

Not on this point, however. On this point, you are the absolute dictator, and your mandate is not subject to compromise or debate. Make the message very clear: tell them they need to achieve and shoot for excellence and they must do it.

Being average is not tolerated. And if they cannot do it or are incapable of achieving this, they need to look elsewhere for work.

CAUTION—BE MINDFUL OF "THE LAW OF ATTRACTION"

We've established that as a top-performing Virtual Boss, the goals your team need to aim for are HIGHER than the goals that the company sets for them. Using this approach, even if they fall short of the goals you have set for them and they have set for themselves, they are still very likely to exceed the company's expectations. It's simple, don't just set the bar high; instead set the bar high**er**.

However, be very careful in how you word all this.

If you have read the book *The Secret*, you know what I mean. The book extensively covers a cornerstone concept of human psychology called The Law of Attraction and how this law has been used by some of the world's greatest minds to achieve the most remarkable achievements in human history.

Simply put, The Law of Attraction states: what you think about, you bring about.

So anything you discuss and think about on a regular basis over time becomes a part of your collective consciousness which in turn becomes your reality. And these things come to you whether you are aware of it or not.

For example:

- If you always talk and think about "lack" of things, then "lack" comes to you.
- If you always talk and think about "abundance" of things, "abundance" comes to you.

This could be for anything: money, health, happiness, results for customers, you name it.

Keeping in mind The Law of Attraction, when setting the bar higher, be careful not to get caught up in the behavior you don't want. Instead, focus largely on the behaviors you do want by concentrating your message on the *desired* outcomes. If you focus too much on the negative, it has a tendency to be attracted to you. Focus on the positive and that will be attracted to you instead.

CHAPTER 5 TAKEAWAYS

» Being a great Virtual Boss requires you to continually challenge your employees to reach higher than they think they are capable of achieving; setting the bar higher rather than high.

» Be "the measuring stick." YOU set the example for your team to follow.

» You are the dictator when it comes to setting the bar higher.

CHAPTER 6
Setting goals

Over fifty years ago, Harvard University performed an interesting study on human behavior and the power of goal setting. The week before the 1954 graduating class were to take their solemn vows of graduation for the very first time and enter the working world in far-flung places around the globe, one hundred of them were gathered by the school's psychology division to take part in a twenty-five-year study.

The study was simple, each of the hundred soon-to-be graduates (they were all men) were interviewed by the staff and asked what they wanted to achieve by the time of their twenty-fifth college reunion.

Prior to the interviews, the Harvard staff randomly assigned the students into two groups. One group would be required to do a post-interview assignment and the other would not be required to do any follow-up.

Each of the students waxed poetically on the pursuits each wanted to pursue, talking of starting successful businesses, achieving advanced degrees, making money on Wall Street and generally achieving varying levels of status, financial gain and professional fulfillment.

The Harvard staff took careful notes, documenting each person's goals and pursuits.

For fifty of them, they not only took notes but asked each one to write down what they had just said about where they would like to be and what they would like to achieve by their twenty-fifth reunion. In essence, they had these people put pen to paper to write out their twenty-five-year goals. The other fifty were free to go after their interview, without being asked to do any further assignment.

Twenty-five years later, the graduates (now alumni) reconvened at the reunion and each individual was interviewed by the Harvard faculty.

What the Harvard researchers uncovered was stunning: the group who had written down their goals had, on average, a net worth which was 197% greater than those of the group who had not set a goal.

One hundred and ninety-seven percent increase in net worth!

That is the power of goals. And this is why they are so integral to your pursuit of being the very best Virtual Boss you can be.

WHY DO GOALS WORK?

Goals subconsciously pre-program the mind to achieve the desired end. Why?

Have you ever been flicking through your cable channels, and come to a movie that looks good, but you have no idea how far through it is? But it looks pretty good so you watch it all the way to the end? A few weeks later you're doing the same thing but this time you catch the movie a little bit earlier, if not right at the very beginning. So you watch it all the way through again because you liked it the first time.

Let me ask you: Did it feel the same the second time around? Were you as wrapped up in the action, sitting on the edge of your seat as you were the first time? Probably not.

This happened to me the first time I saw The Departed —an extremely intense, action-packed movie starring Matt Damon, Jack Nicholson, and Donnie Wahlberg, with an unexpected big plot twist at the end.

When I first watched The Departed, I was so anxious and on the edge of my seat, I could hardly stand it, unsure of exactly how the movie would unravel. I'm usually pretty good at figuring out what the ending will be, but with this one, I really had no idea. The suspense was huge, the plot twists unexpected, and I was totally enthralled.

The second time I watched it, however, it wasn't nearly as good. I was anything but tense. I was relaxed, even indifferent. I realized later that I felt this way because I knew how the movie ended. There was no suspense at all.

Goals do the very same thing. By *knowing how the movie ends*, it enables you to operate in a far more relaxed manner when pursuing the achievement of those goals. Like me watching *The Departed*, you've already seen the movie ending, so it all flows—there's little to no tension.

The point of getting your team to set goals is that after they set them, they have seen the future and they become more relaxed and confident in the achievement of the goal. Because *they have already seen the end of the* movie, your reps' behaviors become automatically self-directed, while being done with greater ease and confidence.

LET *THEM* TELL YOU WHAT *THEY* WANT

You never want to dictate a personal goal to anyone on your staff. They should dictate it to you. You set the tone, as stated at the beginning of this section, but the trick here is to *get them to tell you what they want*. This serves four critical purposes:

1. They feel in control of their destiny.

2. They take full ownership of the task.

3. The goal sends a strong message to them of what can be accomplished in advance of its realization.

4. And best of all, when you pester them about achieving excellence, all you have to remind them is that "You set the goal, not me. I'm just reminding you of what you want!"

It works like magic.

There is nothing more powerful than motivating someone by using their own words repeated back to them.

WHAT ABOUT THE TIME FRAME?

Depending on your organization, set your goals in sync with the organizational structure that you follow.

For example, if your staff work on a monthly, quarterly or annual bonus schedule, then make them do monthly, quarterly, and annual goals. If they are on a quarterly and annual bonus schedule, then goals for quarter and year-end will be fine.

The idea is to keep things as consistent as you can. In essence, set the goal time frame so that they match the payout schedule for your company.

SO HOW DO YOU SET GOALS?

There is a three-step process to successful, motivational goal setting. They are as follows:

1. MAKE THE GOAL SMART

Goals should be five things, and the term used to remember them, which has been adopted by many top and leadership organizations, is "SMART."

SMART stands for:

- specific,
- measurable,
- action-oriented,
- realistic and
- time and resource-constrained.

All five components are critical to the successful accomplishment of a goal. Without one part, the whole goal falls apart. With all five, they work in harmony together to drive the individual towards the goal's ultimate achievement.

Goal setting depends not only on writing a goal statement but also in being able to define the goal clearly.

Another important element to good goal setting is when setting goals, they must be stated in the present tense.

This way, the goal serves a dual purpose: It becomes an affirmation, as well as a stated goal to be achieved. Here's an example of SMART goal setting:

SPECIFIC

The more detail you establish for the goal, the more motivating it becomes.

E.g.: "I'll earn at least $10,000/month." ($10,000 is a specific dollar amount.)

MEASURABLE

A measurable goal establishes a standard for comparison. Doing something "better" or "more accurately" is good, but in order to determine whether you have achieved a goal, you must know how to measure it when it is completed.

E.g.: "I'll earn $120,000 in total pay in 2019." ($120,000 is an extremely measurable quantity.)

ACTION-ORIENTED

Goal statements that produce results usually include action verbs that spur involvement. Such words as "create," "achieve" or "expand" are action verbs.

E.g.: "I'll achieve CEO Circle in 2020." ("Achieve" is a great action word for a goal.)

REALISTIC

For a goal to be motivational, the goal seeker must feel that the goal can be achieved. Impossible goals defeat the goal-setting process. Once your reps feel that a goal is impossible to reach, it becomes difficult for them to mobilize themselves towards its achievement.

E.g.: A goal of "I would like to make $2.7 million in pay in 2019" is certainly a "stretch" goal, but depending on your industry and company, probably a bit unrealistic. "Realistic" goals are those that are "just slightly out of reach" but with a little more effort are attainable. Think of it like reaching for the brass ring on the merry-go-round, it's just slightly out of reach, but only if you could stretch a little bit more then WHAM! You got it! That's what goals should be like.

TIME AND RESOURCE-CONSTRAINED

All goals should have deadlines. On most teams, these deadlines are usually quarterly in a calendar year, as well as year-end. People generally put off doing things if no deadline is set.

E.g.: "I'll achieve Senior Media Buyer by year-end 2020." (Obviously, "year-end 2020" is the definite end to the goal.)

Some examples of potential goal subject matter could be:

- How much monthly compensation they'd like to earn
- Specific personal development goals
- What year-end performance appraisal rating they would like to attain
- What specific training or books they'd like to complete
- What new skills they'd like to acquire

If some members of your staff miss their goals, then you need to follow up. Re-establish why they need to accomplish their goals and why they fell short. Let them know that mediocrity in goal achievement is just as intolerable as mediocrity in goal setting.

For my teams, I have always had them write out a singular goal in advance of each quarter. By the last Friday of each quarter, each team member is to state a SMART goal to me on one sheet of paper for that quarter.

Don't make it too complicated for your reps. Just ensure the goal is centered on their primary area of job responsibility, such as ranking, bonus money and the like.

2. THE 250-WORD ACTION PLAN

Once they determine their goal, simply have them write down their SMART goal on a single sheet of paper. Then below the stated goal have them write in no more than 250 words how they will achieve it.

Tell them to be specific, include legitimate details, and don't let them be vague.

Here's an example of an actual 250-word action plan:

Q3 GOALS

Goal 1:

> » Harvest a data analyzation skill set—this will be one distinct skill set that will make a positive impact on all accounts

> » This is my priority in the next 30 to 60 days, and I've currently purchased these books to get started on harvesting this:

> » *The Model Thinker*

> » *Learn to Think in Systems*

Goal 2:

> » Improve on time management skills

> » So I can also attribute chunks of time to managing different portions of day-to-day account management plus be able to dissect what free time is left, I will review these resources:

- » The 90 Day Year (currently)
- » Ezra's Project Management Course (next on my list)
- » Dan Kennedy's No BS Time Management for Entrepreneurs
- » 18 Minutes
- » The Inefficiency Assassin

Goal 3 (outstanding goal from last quarter):

- » Get better at communication and delegation
- » Utilize Trello boards more often and respond to stuff as it comes in, rather than see it and respond later (which often results in me not responding at all)

Financial Goal:

- » Consistently earn $8K USD/month
- » My ultimate goal is $12K USD/month but my current goal is $8K

What do you need additional training in?

- » Data analysis
- » Communication
- » Time management
- » Delegation

What's your long-term goal and where do you see your role in the agency?

- » My long-term goal is, and always has been,

to be a key person in the agency that people look to for advice and guidance.

> » I know that my individual strengths have always been unique in that I don't always play by the rules to find solutions, however, I find that this leads to innovation and solutions that lie outside the box on a different level.

> » A secondary long-term goal is to hold a position of management or leadership within our agency.

Notice how the goals are specific, the actions are exact and the outcomes are measurable.

It doesn't take long to put this together, but it gives both you and them a roadmap on which you can both work to extract what they want out of their job. It also gives you many opportunities to appropriately deliver Masterful Praisings (more on this later) on every step they take towards achievement.

Best of all, in this above example, the person that put this goal together ended up achieving their goal.

3. SET UP "GOAL REVIEW" DAYS

The next step is to schedule a pre-set day to review the goal as well as a day to review the completion of the goal.

For me, my group and I set a quarterly "Goal-Setting Friday" that is in the last week of the last month of the quarter to set a goal for the following quarter, (for example, June 27 for the third-quarter goal).

We then set a "Goal Review Friday" to review exactly if they achieved their goal. This is scheduled for the first month of each quarter. All of this should be stated ahead of time so the team members know when goal submission is due and the review is to take place. Your time frame should be similar but appropriate for the calendar of events of your organization.

If your company sets goals weekly or monthly, then you can follow a similar schedule in principle.

Set these dates up at your next meeting. Make all of your team commit to the dates in Google calendar. Both dates are KEY to the goal-setting program success. If you just set goals with no follow-up dates, you will forget and the net effect will be lost. Ninety percent of success is knowing and planning to get where you want to go. Goals will help to achieve this as long as you do your part in monitoring it.

Reiterate to them that how they get there (the means) doesn't matter (as long as it doesn't break the law or company policy). Push them to excellence. The most important thing you need to know is the desired end.

To review:

- Set goals using the SMART formula—Specific, Measurable, Action-oriented, Realistic and Time and resource-constrained.

- Record the goal and its action steps on a single sheet of paper. It shouldn't take any more than 250 words for the team member to explain how they are going to achieve their goal.

- Both the individual team member and you keep a copy of that single sheet of paper and review it on a weekly basis during your weekly one-on-one meetings.

- Set dates for "Goal Review" and "Goal Setting"—stick to the schedule and don't miss any days. (If you don't monitor it, they will not proactively do it on their own, and the effect will be lost.)

Once the team member knows what the goal of their job is, there should be no question on what excellent performance looks like. Both sides are clear about what needs to be done.

Remember: you are shooting for PERFECTION and accepting EXCELLENCE!

CHAPTER 6 TAKEAWAYS

» Every employee has a different potential and thus, a different threshold for excellence. You, therefore, must be flexible on how they get themselves there.

» With both short and long-term goals stated, your objectives are far easier to achieve.

» After your employees set goals, they have seen the future and become more relaxed in goal achievement.

» Your employees dictate their goals to you because there is nothing more powerful than motivating someone by using their own words repeated back to motivate them.

» Set your goals in sync with the organizational timeline you follow. Be aligned with the company payout schedule.

» Have your employees set quarterly (or whatever time frame is most appropriate) goals:

> » Make them SMART (Specific, Measurable, Action-oriented, Realistic, Time and resource-constrained)

> » One goal with a 250 word or less Action Plan

> » Review goal weekly

> » Plan goal review days at end of each quarter

CHAPTER 7
Beware! The downside of goals

Among psychologists, the link between setting goals and achievement is one of the clearest there is. There are wide-ranging studies like our Harvard example that prove that we as humans concentrate better, work longer and do more if we set SMART-type goals for ourselves.

However, there is a dark side to goalsetting. As a top-performing Virtual Boss, you need to be aware of this downside. There is recent evidence that individuals, companies and governments can hurt themselves by blindly following goals, although they may seem to make a whole lot of sense at the time of creation.

The evidence shows that goals, although well-intended, can restrain our thinking and create an effect that is opposite to the one we want.

It is not that goal setting does not work, because it does.

It's just that goal setting, if not done correctly, can focus attention on the wrong things; it can lead to behaviors that are not healthy and can be destructive.

PRESCRIPTION-STRENGTH GOALS

It is well documented that when people are told to "do their best," they more often than not, do not.

However, when people have specific goals that energize them, it keeps them engaged for longer. Great companies such as General Electric (GE) and Southwest Airlines have used goals to energize their employees around a central purpose, pulling off amazing feats of managerial genius in the process.

Adam Galinsky, a professor at the Kellogg School of Management at Northwestern University cautions this, however:

> "Goal setting has been treated like an over-the-counter medication when it should really be treated with more care, as a prescription-strength medication."

Although goals brought us great successes from companies such as GE and Southwest, goals also brought us spectacular failures from Enron and General Motors, two companies whose failures occurred in spite of well-meaning and ambitious goals.

The problem is this; recent data shows that if people are close to their goals or are in fear of missing their goals, they are more likely to lie to make up the difference.

For example, the recent dysfunctional environment at Enron came about via its practice of rewarding top-level executives on meeting revenue targets. This had a direct correlation to the criminal activity that ultimately led to the downfall and eventual bankruptcy of the firm.

In another example, in the mid-1990s, Sears, Roebuck and Co began setting revenue goals for its service staff, only to realize that its mechanics were overcharging and making unnecessary repairs to unwitting customers so that they hit their numbers.

Yikes.

BEWARE OF THE "B-HAG"

Further, the study from Kellogg found that "stretch goals" were also in jeopardy of losing their luster. They found that more often than not these kinds of goals were pursued by desperate companies—the ones most likely ill-prepared to deal with their ultimate failures.

They found that these are the companies that issue "Big Hairy Audacious Goals" (called "B-Hags" for short). Their research found that the setting of these goals are just desperate attempts to create something out of nothing, and are more often than not, doomed to failure from the start.

(Having lived through a corporate "B-Hag" myself, I couldn't agree more.)

FOCUS VS TUNNEL VISION

In a famous study on how well people perform certain tasks by Daniel Simons and Christopher Chabris, participants were told to count how many times a group of individuals passed a ball between them. Because they were so focused on counting the passes, the study participants never saw a woman in a gorilla suit passing in plain view through the middle of the group!

(I will admit that I did this in a management training program and never saw the gorilla-suited woman!)

It's definitely true that a simple goal can lead to bursts of intense effort in the short term. However, the risk is that those short-term gains may also undermine the long-term interests of the individual.

This is why it's so important to attain harmonious short and long-term goals that are codependent on each other. Take for example, the dieter who resumes smoking to help lose that last 20 pounds. This is not exactly short-term and long-term goal harmony!

The challenge is that when you set goals, be very careful what behavior you are rewarding.

FILTER FOR MISALIGNMENT

When your team members come to you with their finalized goals, ask yourself if their goals are in line with what you feel is possible for each individual. Is the goal a jumble of hyperbole just to satisfy the boss? Or does it actually have some real meaning and substance? Is it possible for the goal to be reached? Or will there be some "fudging" along the way to make it seem like it has been achieved?

You as a top-performing Virtual Boss must be the one who safeguards the entire process while being mindful that there is a downside to overly ambitious goals. Overly ambitious "stretch goals" can lead to illicit or even illegal behavior, so be wary of this and safeguard against it in your editing.

You don't want your team venturing into the dark side, for if they do, both of you are responsible.

A good creed to keep in mind: If the goals are too elaborate, then knock them back down; aggressive goals are good, but realistic ones are far better. With your careful guidance, you can help protect your team from themselves and prevent the downside of goalsetting.

CHAPTER 7 TAKEAWAYS

» Goals can restrain our thinking and create an effect that is opposite to the one we want.

» Set harmonious short and long-term goals that are codependent on each other to decrease the likelihood of cheating or lying to achieve the goal.

» Your careful guidance can help protect your employees from themselves and prevent the downside of goal setting.

ACTION GUIDE

SET THE BAR HIGHER

How will YOU communicate your "setting the bar higher" message to YOUR team?

Write down your own versions of "setting the bar higher statements."

_____

_____

_____

_____

_____

_____

_____

_____

_____

_____

_____

_____

_____

Make sure those statements are focused on "abundance" and not "lack."

Now create a plan for delivering these messages (i.e. during weekly meetings with the team, a weekly email to the team, a daily text message to the team), all or a combination of all of the above.

_____

_____

_____

_____

_____

_____

_____

_____

_____

_____

_____

_____

_____

ASSESS YOUR TEAM MEMBERS

Using a list of your people, assess them using the following parameters:

1. Who needs to just meet their goal (i.e. those who have never achieved a goal before) and who needs to far exceed their goals?

2. Rank them in terms of talent and/or skill.

GOAL-HITTING TEAM MEMBERS:

NAME	RANK

GOAL-BUSTING TEAM MEMBERS:

NAME	RANK

Based on the above list, come up with your idea for each team member's quarterly goal and note it in the table on the next page. This will assist you in playing the editor-in-chief role when they come to you with their goals.

NAME	GOAL

SECTION 2 – FINAL REFLECTION

Based on the previous exercises and what you've learned in this section, what do you need to improve on to be a better Virtual Boss?

_____

_____

_____

_____

_____

_____

_____

_____

SECTION 3

HOW TO MOTIVATE YOUR TEAM TO PEAK PERFORMANCE

HOW TO MOTIVATE YOUR TEAM TO PEAK PERFORMANCE

There are so many management gurus who have written tomes and dissertations on exactly how to motivate people, all in search of the "one thing" that does it all with minimal effort.

The real truth is that there is no ONE way to do it.

Motivating people in a way that triggers explosive growth is the sum of hundreds, if not thousands of small decisions that you make on a daily basis.

Here's the tricky thing: Since motivating people effectively does not amount to any ONE thing, you need to know how to coalesce all these actions into a cohesive, well-oiled machine. And when this is all done precisely right, it will result in a motivated new hire who is willing to go through walls for both themselves and for you.

Do you blindly follow "the Golden Rule"?

Because the Golden Rule says that you should "treat others as you would like to be treated." It says that being fair and treating everyone the same is what being a great boss is all about. Makes sense, right?

For example, when you were doing their job, perhaps you were primarily motivated by money. So conventional thinking would dictate this means your whole staff is driven by money too, right?

This is precisely the kind of flawed thinking that the average Virtual Boss falls into. If you motivate your team around the very same objectives that YOU felt were important when you were in their job, that is conventional virtual management, and conventional thinking is what we are trying to avoid.

Every person you are managing is different so it's pointless trying to motivate them all the same.

What you really need to do is *get to know them* in order to truly appreciate how different each one is, then celebrate these differences!

So how do you harness each individual's different motivations in order to achieve peak performance? There will be a different motivator or trigger for each one, and you have to find out what that trigger is. The good news is, this information is relatively easy to get.

Also, you really need to be mindful of WHO you are motivating, because that's as, if not more, important than HOW you are motivating. You see, this motivating thing isn't that easy. It's actually the hardest thing to do as a boss and manager. And it's even harder to do REALLY well.

Here's a big clue though. EVERYTHING you do as a boss: Every email, Zoom call, phone call and text message must congruently align your message with an undercurrent of motivation. In everything you do, you must be motivating and communicating for a specific reason. And that reason is to unleash superior results from your staff members.

That is your ONLY (and most important) goal.

Now let's dive in.

CHAPTER 8

Peel back the onion

"Being fair" is what being a great boss is all about. Or so say the traditional methods of management. When you were doing your staff's job, you were primarily motivated by money. This means that your staff members are all driven by money, right?

This is precisely what the average Virtual Boss does, but you are not average.

This conventional thinking is deeply flawed; the extraordinary Virtual Boss knows that each person is truly different. If you treat them all the same, then peak performance is impossible to achieve.

Think about it, just because you like something and hold it dear, does that mean others do the same? For your spouse's birthday, did you present her with a 42 inch plasma TV because that is what you wanted? Or did you present him with a set of 2 karat diamond earrings because that is what you wanted? Of course not.

PEOPLE ARE DIFFERENT

As the saying goes:

"There are a million ways to make a million dollars."

Likewise, there are millions of ways in which a team member can be successful. I've never met two that are exactly the same and I'm sure you haven't either.

Instead of railing against those differences, celebrate them.

Each person has their own individual triggers for success, things that make them uniquely different. And those motivations are far different for each one.

So how do you harness each individual's different motivations in order to achieve peak performance?

DON'T GET TOO COMPLICATED

The first thing you need to do is find out *what actually motivates them.*

So how do you do it? Do you hypnotize them? Do you ask roundabout questions on what they were like when they were children? Do you ask them questions about their personal lives (are they getting married soon, are they looking to buy a house, do they want to just stay single)? Do you perform psychoanalysis on them and ask them about their deepest darkest secrets, their father and their mother, uncovering complexes and "mommy never loved me" scenarios? Do you call their past bosses and interview them?

You don't need to do any of that.

In fact, what you need to do is so simple. You simply ask.

I am truly amazed at how many bosses have no idea what motivates their team members. In fact, just the other day a colleague of mine was telling me about a problem team member of hers and how he "doesn't do this and he doesn't do that …"

So I asked her, "What motivates him?"

She stammered and stuttered and clearly made up something on the spot like "money, uh, I think."

I thought, how can she possibly expect to get this person to do anything if she has NO IDEA what makes him tick?

We all do it, though. We all get so caught up in all the emails and conference calls and signing off on expense reports and monitoring the administrative tasks—all the things that get in the way of actually doing the single most important thing that we need to know about our team members. We need to know what gets them out of bed in the morning. What makes them tick? What drives them?

You need to get this information from your team. Otherwise, you are flying blind. If you want to get the best from your people and push them to achieve excellence then you need to know what drives them to get themselves there.

It doesn't matter how you get your information, all you need to do is get it. Then as soon as you get it, keep it in their file and refer to it at every chance you can get. Remind yourself constantly of what makes that person tick.

Use that information as a daily guide to steer your conversations and interactions with them. The goal is to give them what they want, not what you think they should want. By asking them what they want and not what you think they want, you lower your own filter and release yourself from your own biases.

Let your team tell you what their triggers are. Then simply gear your interactions to perfectly match those triggers.

THE TEN QUESTIONS

Here are the Ten Questions I ask my individual team members:

1. What drives you?
2. What are the barriers standing in your way of ultimate success?
3. What are you shooting for in your current position?
4. How do you get paid?
5. Where do you see your career heading?
6. How do you like to be praised? Do you like it publicly, privately, written or verbal?
7. What's the most significant recognition you have ever received? Why was it so memorable?
8. What are you best at?
9. What were the qualities of your best ever boss?
10. What were the qualities of your worst ever boss?

There's a reason why each of these questions is asked. There are specific motivations hidden in the wording of each.

The point is that when you get this information, you have "the golden ticket." In the movie *Willy Wonka and the Chocolate Factory*, Charlie finds the golden ticket and he gets the key to the tour of the factory with all the grandeur and happiness it provides. He feels like anything is possible; that the sky's the limit!

With this information, the sky's the limit with you as well.

Here are some ideas to get the information you need:

- Perhaps at your next meeting, before you start your presentation, send a link to a Google doc with the Ten Questions and get your team members to answer them.

- Or, when you get a chance later tonight after reading this, cut and paste the Ten Questions and email them to your team members. Tell them you would like the answers back in two days.

- Or maybe do it individually. The next time you're on your weekly one-on-ones with them, have the Ten Questions available and ask them. Then tell them you're going to write down their answers so you have them. Your people will give the answers to you. All you need to do is ask.

Whatever you do, however, don't ask them at Performance Review time; just ask them casually in the normal flow of business. They'll be far more open about it this way.

In fact, by asking them the Ten Questions, you will be making a huge deposit into their Trust Account as you are showing them you truly care about them and are going above and beyond what any former boss may have done to figure out what makes them tick.

Remember that without this information you are totally and completely blind. But with it, you have some of the most precious insights into how to motivate your team members.

Awareness of these things is half the battle. Once you know, all you need to do is start using it so you can unleash the best from them.

CHAPTER 8 TAKEAWAYS

» The extraordinary Virtual Boss knows that each person is truly different. If you treat them all the same, then peak performance is impossible to achieve.

» Find out what motivates each individual employee by asking them the Ten Questions.

» Use the information you gather from asking the Ten Questions as a daily guide to steer your conversations and interactions with your employees.

CHAPTER 9

More of what's already there

In his book First, Break All the Rules, Marcus Buckingham ponders the thought: *can each person truly be anything they want to be if they just set their mind to it?*

In line with this, what you need to ask yourself as a top-performing Virtual Boss is: *is it possible for each of my individual team members to be the #1 in the company?*

The romantic story is that yes, anything is achievable as long as you set your mind to it. It's so uplifting, it's so optimistic, it's so … not possible.

THE FABLE IS NOT TRUE

We have read these fables as children. You are told from a very early age that you have unlimited potential. *"You can do whatever you set your mind to,"* says the old expression. *"What the mind can conceive, it can achieve,"* says another one.

Do you actually believe this?

My father used to say to us as kids that "we live in the greatest country in the world because any kid can grow up to become president of the United States."

Was Dad actually right or is this just a happy bedtime story that makes kids feel good about themselves just as they drift off to sleep at night?

> "Work hard at school, get good grades, do what mom and dad tell you, and you too can become President someday."

The question then is: do we all, as humans, have the exact same potential?

Or more pointedly: does each of your staff have the exact same potential?

The real truth is that each individual has *differing levels of potential*. This is not really new news, due largely to the fact that each of us has different genetic codes that dictate at an early age what we have tendencies and propensities for.

For example, some of us are good at math at an early age. Some of us have great timing and a sense of humor. Some have an inherent sense of creativity, some have intense energy, some are cool under fire, some are exacting and precise; the list goes on and on.

I know this is crushing news to those bosses hoping to seek higher office but, not anyone can be president of the United States (or, if you don't live in the USA, insert your country-appropriate "highest office in the land" here). I know I could never be president. I simply don't have the desire or the energy. Moreover, I don't have the genetic makeup necessary to tolerate a two-year election process nor the intellectual horsepower to run the most powerful country in the world.

Likewise, not everyone can be great. There are plenty of people who can be good. We have loads of them in the world. In fact, you probably have a few on your team now. However, in order to be truly great, you have to possess certain innate talents.

A great team member can learn skills or gain experience that will augment his talents and elevate them to turn in an excellent performance, but skills alone will never elevate a struggling staff member to excellence. They need the skills that equate to success.

TALENTS? SKILLS? WHAT'S THE DIFFERENCE?

There's a big difference. A difference you need to be able to identify in individuals both in interviews as well as staff members who you may have inherited from other bosses so that you can use this understanding to propel your team to true excellence.

In *First, Break All the Rules*, Marcus Buckingham states:

> Talent is "Nature."
> Skill is "Nurture."

TALENTS

Talents are inherent, genetically encoded patterns of thought and behavior.

For example, self-confidence is a talent, you either have it or you don't. Can a person learn self-confidence? You might be able to make your team slightly more self-confident in certain situations through some of the techniques we'll discover in this program. But can you create self-confidence in your people? This is highly unlikely and nearly impossible.

Further, some people have self-confidence only when they are performing certain activities. This is referred to as *performance confidence*. For example, the defensive back (yes, another football analogy) who hoots and hollers when he is breaking up passes on the football field has performance confidence when he's playing. That same defensive back, when it comes time to explain his feats in front of the media gathered after the game, suddenly becomes shy and awkward.

He has performance confidence on the field of play, but in other circumstances, he does not.

"Strong drive to succeed" is a talent as well. Some of us are just naturally driven to achieve, and others are just naturally lazy. There are a million points all along the continuum from over-the-top driven to deadbeat lazy. But you can't teach someone to be driven, unfortunately. You can place them in an environment in which they are more driven than in other environments, but at the core of it all, they either have that trait or they do not.

For example, I would consider myself a fairly driven person. However, I work in a field that I'm extremely passionate about. If I worked in a field in which I had no passion for whatsoever, (like, say, the tire industry), I would have little to no real drive. No matter how hard I tried, I would never be able to work myself into a froth first thing in the morning to go out and sell a set of Goodyear Eagle Ultra Grip GW-3s. It would just never happen for me.

My point is this, your staff are all "driven to succeed" at certain degrees along the continuum and they all have differing levels of "self-confidence and charisma" as well. Some have more, some have less.

So when it comes to motivating your team, you as a top-performing Virtual Boss can draw more of these talents out of them—but you cannot instill these talents in them. Let me say that again because it is important:

You as a top-performing Virtual Boss can draw more of their talents out of them—but you cannot instill these talents there in the first place.

The key talents for success need to be "in their genetic code" for your staff member to achieve success. Barring a brain transplant, it will be a long, long road for the both of you as you wait and wait to finally see them succeed. If the key talents needed for success are not there in the first place, then you can try and take some corrective action.

Before we do that, however, we need to understand the key differences between talents and its oftentimes confused counterpart, skills.

SKILLS

Unlike talents, skills are things that can be taught by you, the top-performing Virtual Boss. This is one of your key responsibilities.

For example, knowledge of a product or class of products and services is a skill. Oftentimes termed "industry experience," it's always good to have a person that you don't have to teach the basics of an industry and its jargon because they have worked in the same or similar industry for a few years. This is certainly attractive to have in a team member. Not essential, but attractive.

In fact, all things that can either be learned or can be duplicated over and over, passed along from one to the next are skills. Industry experience can be taught, yes. However, this is a long process, as I'm sure you know. Nonetheless, it is a skill acquired through firsthand knowledge. Industry experience, although it is a lengthy process, can be passed from one person to the next.

A skill example from my sales management days is mastery of the five stages of a sales call. Knowing the five phases of opening, investigating (probing), proposing (pitching), overcoming objections, closing are all steps that can be learned.

However, *having the innate sense to know at which point and exactly when to do each step, as well as how smoothly and effortlessly it is all done is a talent.* This is a key distinction. The fact that they know it is not good enough for you. The fact that *they have mastery over it* is very valuable to you.

In other words, the process can be taught. However, the subtleties of how it's implemented and the effectiveness thereof, are talents.

DON'T BE DECEIVED BY LAZY THINKING

First things first, you must hire for talents that are essential for the achievement of excellence. You can teach skills, but you cannot teach talents. They're either there or they are not.

This then begs the question: Can a person truly change themselves by working at it? Can a person that lacks "drive to succeed" truly change themselves at the core, by going to classes and doing extra study? If this premise is actually true, then this proposes we are all the same. And you know as well as I do that no two people are the same.

Have you managed people that no matter how good they become, no matter how much they work at it, you know that they'll never achieve top performance? No matter how hard they study, how much they work at it, they'll never be at that level. You know it deep down, but hold fast to the statement that if they set their mind to it, they can become great?

Top-performing Virtual Bosses know that this simply is not true. Although the idea is romantic, they realize that not only is it unrealistic, but it's far too awkward. The top bosses know that each person has a finite limit of their individual potential. They understand inherently that talents and weaknesses limit each person's ability to achieve mastery and ultimate excellence.

Top-performing Virtual Bosses know that inherent talents of individuals can be coaxed, coached, prodded and cultivated to bring out small incremental gains in efficiency from those talents. They also know that if a team member does not possess enough of the talent essential for success, or if it's completely absent, then the true potential for that person will be far more limited than those who do possess such talents in great quantity.

At the heart of it all, the top-performing boss knows that a "weakness" cannot be taught, coached or coaxed in, no matter how good a motivator or leader they are. In fact, it's the *mediocre* Virtual Boss who is so delusional that they actually think that they can change a person at their core.

As Marcus Buckingham says in *First, Break All the Rules*: "*People don't change a whole lot.*"

In our case, your team members don't change a whole lot.

It's the top-performing Virtual Boss who cuts their losses and moves onward to termination if they realize the person, no matter how hard they try, will never "get it."

It's also the top-performing Virtual Boss who *maximizes* strengths and *minimizes* weaknesses in their team members.

THE REAL GLASS CEILING

Picture if you will, an invisible glass ceiling over each one of your staff.

The ceiling height is limited by the amount of talent each possesses for ultimate success in their role. This ceiling height is determined by the inherent limitations they have when it comes to the qualities necessary for ultimate success. Can a person who lacks or is deficient in certain core talents for the job ever be hugely successful? The answer is no.

As a rule, there are far more differences between individual high-performing staff members than there are similarities.

The average Virtual Boss believes that if they diligently work on each individual person's weaknesses, trying desperately to get them to make up for their weaknesses through hard work and extra effort, they'll eventually turn them around and be successful. The boss sends them to conferences, has them do remedial training, all in the hope that the person will eventually turn their weaknesses into strengths to achieve the associated enhanced performance.

At performance appraisal time, the average Virtual Boss spends the majority of time talking about the areas of opportunity for each team member, hoping and believing that if the person "just improved a few things," then they could achieve even better performance.

In direct contrast to the average boss who tries to fix each person's weaknesses, top-performing Virtual Bosses work to draw out more of their talents—namely those things they are good at. Top bosses highlight those talents that catalyze success in the role while minimizing weaknesses.

PLAY TO THEIR STRENGTHS

The best, high-performing bosses observe their team. They notice that each individual has certain core talents. They make mental notes of their team's strengths as well as their weaknesses. They know they can leverage their talents as a launching point to coax even greater performance out of their individual staff members.

For example, let's compare two top-performing people, in this case, two salespeople, both having achieved the highest awards in their companies with great track records of success.

"Jane" has an incredible talent for building rapport, easily weaving pleasant conversation in a goal-oriented manner. Jane's manner is easygoing and laid-back but hides a profound inner drive. She is completely in control of the situation at all times and asks many-layered questions of the prospect to uncover their needs. Instead of being "all business," she talks about jewellery, kids and other non-business activities; easily mixing in rapport building with working throughout the process. She doesn't take herself too seriously and takes time for some self-deprecating asides while constantly driving towards the sale. She uses no real reference pieces. Instead, she relies on her easy, trustworthy manner to build credibility and assume the close of the sale.

In contrast, "Tom" is incredibly persistent. He is a little bit awkward in his approach, but people respect him due to his aggressiveness and "never taking no for an answer" mentality. When he is in a meeting, he's all business with no rapport building whatsoever but asks a few precisely worded questions to uncover the customer's needs. Just like his initial approach, when he hears objections, he assertively asks the reasons behind the objections, then pulls out reference materials to overcome the objections and validate his ideas and claims. At the end of the sale, he asks alternate close questions, awaits responses before proceeding and aggressively pushes for the next step, and is very successful in doing so.

Would you as the boss of both Jane and Tom look at the above scenarios and think to yourself: "if I could just get Jane to use more reference materials and ask more hard questions, she would really be even better!"

Or would you think: "Tom's just too rough, I need to get him to soften up his hard edge and build more rapport. He also needs to ask more questions to uncover needs."

In both cases, you would be falling into the most common, yet well-meaning trap that average bosses make. You would be trying to perfect them, and I have news for you ... your efforts will be futile.

You could be Mohandas Gandhi and you still would not be able to change Jane and Tom too much. In fact, neither will change a whole lot their entire lives. Their styles are different but effective, so why try to change them?

When it comes to this, average bosses make the mistake of doing two things very consistently, they:

1. Focus on fixing their team members' weaknesses.
2. Try (in a desperate and futile attempt) to get their people to be more like themselves.

You'll never get Jane to be more like Tom and you'll never get Tom to be more like Jane. And further, you'll never get Jane or Tom to ever be like you.

So why try?

What a top-performing Virtual Boss does is push their people to be even BETTER at the things they are good at, while minimizing the things they are not so good at.

In each case, all of those character traits mentioned for Jane and Tom are "talents." In the case of Jane, her rapport building, easygoing manner of questioning and self-deprecating humor are all talents. Tom's serious yet determined drive, his resilience and his closing ability and timing are all talents.

The top-performing boss would look at the two of them and use those talents as the foundation to build, and then further augment each individual person's performance. The top-performing boss would constantly refer to these talents—even when they are being reprimanded for something unrelated.

In the case of Jane, let's say you're strategizing with her before a meeting. You would give her some instructions like this:

> "Since you build rapport so easily and ask such great non-threatening questions, you may want to approach presenting your ideas in the meeting this way ..."

In the case of Tom, say you're on the phone with him going through his latest customer presentation. You would share:

"Because you're so great at getting your main points across and because people immediately have respect for your persistence, I would …"

In both cases, you're building them up. You're referring to their talents and using that talent to launch into how you may want to proceed with the particular endeavor you're discussing with them at that time. This could be just a passing conversation or it could be in a formal strategy session. Either one works.

What you're doing is you're drawing out their talents.

So let's review.

First, identify their talents. Then make mention of their talents in your discussions with each team member. This motivates them to be more of who they are. You build rapport, trust and respect with them in the process.

But most importantly, they feel like you're *accepting them for who they are* instead of you trying to make them who they are not.

THE BAD RELATIONSHIP

I'm sure you've been in bad relationships like this in the past: The ones where the partner, although they may like you, is always trying to make you someone who you are not. This constant nipping at your ego and self-worth dooms the relationship for failure.

Those same "quirks" that in the first part of the dating scene were amusing and charming have lost their luster. Now, these are no longer "quirks," they're annoyances. The constant chipping away at each other's character flaws makes neither party happy anymore; and after many knock-down, drag-out fights, the relationship ends.

Don't let this happen to you as a top-performing Virtual Boss. For your average "meet the goal" team members or even for your top "goal-busting" team members, the procedure is the same: uncover their talents, and then leverage these strengths as launch pads for even better performance.

Back to *First, Break All the Rules*, in essence, this means:

> "Draw out more of what they have, instead of trying to fix what they don't."

It's far easier to do it this way than the reverse. And it's far more satisfying for both you and them.

CHAPTER 9 TAKEAWAYS

» Not every one of your employees can be the top employee in the company.

» A great employee can learn skills or gain experience that will augment their talents and elevate them to turn in excellent performance, but skills alone will never elevate a struggling employee to excellence.

» TALENTS are inherent, genetically encoded patterns of thought and behavior (nature).

» SKILLS are learned abilities that can be passed along from person to person through instruction (nurture).

» You as a top-performing Virtual Boss can draw more of their talents out of your employees—but you cannot instill them in there in the first place.

» Unlike talents, skills are things that can be taught by you, the top-performing boss.

» A top-performing boss pushes their employees to be even BETTER at the things they are good at while minimizing the things they are not so good at.

» Identify your employees' talents, then inject them and make mention of them in your discussions with them.

CHAPTER 10

A person who feels good about themselves produces better work

When do you do your best work?

Is it when you feel *bad* or is it when you feel *good*?

The fairly obvious answer is when you feel good. No one feels like doing much of anything when they feel bad.

So it begs the question: does the person brimming with confidence produce higher quality work than the person who lacks confidence?

The answer may seem obvious, but why do so few managers spend the majority of their time building their people's confidence up instead of ripping it down?

It could be that many bosses have done their team's jobs themselves prior to becoming the manager and employ the "seagull management" approach (swoop in, dump on the person, then fly away), and that is all they know about management.

In this case, unfortunately, ignorance begets more ignorance.

I'm not sure why this is (having been managed by quite a few seagulls), but I do know that this management style is way too common and largely ineffective for creating superior results.

A TALE TO REMEMBER

Many years ago in London, England there lived a boy whose parents had abandoned him. He lived in a small hovel with seven other boys, pasting labels on bottles during the day and scavenging for food at night, oftentimes going to bed hungry.

In spite of the hardship, this boy longed to be a writer for great notoriety and fame. In his spare hours, he wrote many manuscripts and submitted them to the local newspapers for consideration. He often ran out in the middle of the night to mail the manuscripts off, having such little confidence in his ability to be successful and so shameful of his failures. Story after story after story was refused.

Then one day an editor accepted his story. He did not get paid for it, but he had finally been recognized for doing good work. The words of the publisher made him so happy that he walked around the city for hours in a daze, tears streaming from his eyes of pure joy. If it had not been for that one editor finally recognizing him and his talents, we may never have the treasured works he produced in the years after. In fact, the recognition he received from that one editor changed his life and gave him the self-esteem and confidence to continue on and subsequently write many of the great novels of our time.

The boy's name was Charles Dickens.

Sometimes, motivating people can be just that simple.

Do you want to know how to motivate your team? There is no magic formula. Doing basic, simple constructive things to get them moving in the right direction is all you need to do.

Everyone, from the CEO of the largest corporation to the sales clerk at the grocery store, to one of your unappreciated team members wants to be told that they are doing a first-class job. They all *crave* recognition.

One of the greatest human needs is the need for recognition. It's as important to them as the air they breathe.

Just a little bit of encouragement or a splash of recognition at precisely the right moment is sometimes all it takes to transform a good team member into a great team member.

This concept was ingrained in me at an early stage of my sales management career with one of my relatively new salespeople. We had a morning appointment with a client and a full slate of calls for what was a very busy sales day.

At our first appointment, my salesperson approached the front desk and the office manager appeared, stating that the client would be coming in late and he would not be able to meet with us. Even though the client didn't want to see us, my salesperson somehow managed to work her way to the back office, where she knew she could access a colleague of the client who had great influence in the office and secret access to the client.

Sure enough, despite the client's objection to "not having enough time" and "being behind," my salesperson got in front of him, and asked him about his needs, gaining a full understanding of his business issues. Based on her questioning, she suddenly realized he "had time" to speak with us.

She then made her pitch using all the information she had just gathered, perfectly tailoring her offering to his unique needs and gained his commitment.

As we left the office, it was clear my salesperson was bubbling with excitement at the outcome of the meeting, clearly happy with the outcome. As was I.

As we were about to get in her car and drive to the next appointment, I stopped, turned to her and said:

> "You are really good. In fact, you are going to be hugely successful in this company performing like you just did. I really mean it, you made that meeting—the one that almost didn't happen—successful. You uncovered his needs, went through our services and how they would help his business perform better based on that discussion. It was just great. It's especially impressive considering your limited four-month tenure with us."

I could just see her glow.

That glow lasted all day long. It lasted into every other meeting we had that day.

At the end of the day, she turned to me, clearly reflecting on the day and wondered aloud:

> "This was such a great day we had together today, why is it that whenever we ride together, we have such great days?"

I think I have an idea why.

What did I do?

All I really did was reference her considerable talents and told her how much I appreciate her efforts.

I'm no genius, don't get me wrong. All I know is that whenever I was working with her, I made it a point to make her *feel good about herself*.

Your job as a boss is to recognize this in your team members then call it out. When your team feels good, feels confident and feels like what they do matters, they produce big-time results for you.

FEEL GOOD = PRODUCE MORE

This may be the basics of Management 101, but the person who feels good, produces more; it's just that simple. People perform better under a feeling of appreciation and praise than they do under a feeling of criticism and negativity.

If you make them feel important and make them feel good about what they are doing on a day-to-day basis, then you'll be on the path to superior results. Sometimes all it takes from you is just a few words to let them know that you appreciate what they do.

You may believe that the only thing that all your staff members are interested in is money as their reward.

However, even the most materialistic of us know that there are more important rewards than money alone.

The two rewards that top the list are self-respect and the respect of others.

People love to feel important, needed and respected in the workplace, so your job as a top-level Virtual Boss is to create an environment in which your people experience those feelings in a genuine manner. Seek out opportunities to tell them that you appreciate what they are doing. In doing so, you will find that the work and results you receive in return come back to you tenfold.

You need to know how to do it though. This is important.

"Hey Tom, you did a good job on that."

OK, that's praise, but it's empty praise. It really means nothing.

As an old boss once told me:

"If praise ain't specific, it ain't terrific."

Vague praise is so meaningless you may as well not even bother. In fact, you may do more harm than good. With specific praise, you get people to do more of what you want.

Remember, when you're operating a virtual company, you're not with your staff members 95 percent of the time they're working. So it's important to get them to be willing to act on their own in the right way independent of your presence. And you can do that by praising what they do well (so they do more of it).

In the next chapter, we'll dive deeper into exactly how to praise.

CHAPTER 10 TAKEAWAYS

» The employee who feels good produces more; it's just that simple. People perform better under a feeling of appreciation and praise than they do under a feeling of criticism and negativity.

» There are more important rewards than money alone. Two rewards that top the list are self-respect and the respect of others.

» Seek out opportunities to tell your employees that you appreciate what they are doing.

» "If praise ain't specific, it ain't terrific."

CHAPTER 11
Masterful Praisings

"A pat on the back is only a few vertebrae removed from a kick in the pants, but is miles ahead in results."
–ELLA WHEELER WILCOX

After your team set their goals, the next most important motivational step follows. This is not high science, it is not groundbreaking, but the simplest solutions to issues are often the most elegant.

Let me ask you. Do you remember the last praise you received from someone at work?

I'll bet you do.

Motivating others is as simple as praising team members for specific acts of excellence. We call them Masterful Praisings. After you and your team set your SMART goals and they write them out in 250 words or less, keep a watchful eye on them.

CATCH YOUR STAFF DOING THE RIGHT THING

When new goals are created for each quarter, you need to stay in very close contact with your individual staff members, communicating with them via whatever communication vehicles your company has in place (Slack, project management software, instant message, email, phone).

The purpose of all this is to "catch them" doing something right as often as possible.

There is an art to this, however.

The *best* Virtual Bosses praise their staff members when they do something *on the way* to getting it right.

The *average* Virtual Boss waits until an individual staff member does something *exactly right* before they give *any* praise.

As a result of this, most people never become high performers because their boss focuses on criticizing instead of encouraging.

After receiving no feedback and getting criticized frequently, people may not know what correct behavior even looks like. They end up not producing or "pushing paper" all day long. After all, it's too hard to do anything because of the fear of being punished. They think: "why take the risk of doing anything because if I get it wrong the boss is just gonna come down on me?"

What the average boss does with a new hire is welcome them in, introduce them to their co-workers, then leave them alone. In this unfortunate scenario, the only attention that the new hire gets is occasional criticism or very little feedback on results.

This is what is wrong with most organizations; much of the reason for poor performance is because the people are led so poorly.

USING GOALS TO GUIDE YOUR MASTERFUL PRAISINGS

If inexperienced team members don't perform well, instead of criticizing, go back to the masterful goal-setting document you created with them in Section 2.

This document is essential for setting the bar higher, but this document is perhaps even more powerful as a motivational tool for praising them when something is done nearly right.

Let's use our 250-word action plan example from Section 2 as an example.

Q3 GOALS

Goal 1:

> » Harvest a data analyzation skill set—this will be one distinct skill set that will make a positive impact on all accounts

> » This is my priority in the next 30 to 60 days, and I've currently purchased these books to get started on harvesting this:

> » *The Model Thinker*

> » *Learn to Think in Systems*

Goal 2:

> » Improve on time management skills

> » So I can also attribute chunks of time to managing different portions of day-to-day account management plus be able to dissect what free time is left, I will review:

>> » The 90 Day Year (currently)

>> » Ezra's Project Management Course (next on my list)

>> » Dan Kennedy's No BS Time Management for Entrepreneurs

>> » 18 Minutes

>> » The Inefficiency Assassin

Goal 3 (outstanding goal from last quarter):

> » Get better at communication and delegation

» Utilize Trello boards more often and respond to stuff as it comes in, rather than see it and respond later (which often results in me not responding at all)

Financial Goal

» Consistently earn $8K USD/month

» My ultimate goal is $12K USD/month but my current goal is $8K

What do you need additional training in?

» Data analysis

» Communication

» Time management

» Delegation

What's your long-term goal and where do you see your role in the agency?

» My long-term goal is, and always has been, to be a key person in the agency that people look to for advice and guidance.

» I know that my individual strengths have always been unique in that I don't always play by the rules to find solutions, however, I find that this leads to innovation and solutions that lie outside the box on a different level.

» A secondary long-term goal is to hold a position of management or leadership within our agency.

There are multiple opportunities to deliver many Masterful Praisings here.

When any of these tasks on this document are completed, even the small ones, the time is right for a Masterful Praising.

The great boss is always vigilant in looking for, as well as creating situations, (especially at the beginning of an assignment) where they can deliver a Masterful Praising.

Goals not only create a roadmap for success for the team member, but they also provide you, as the boss, a 250-word document chock full of potential Masterful Praisings.

When the staff member performs any of the steps on that plan, whether it be nearly or exactly correct, deliver the Masterful Praising on the spot.

If you need to, get on a specific call to your team member with no other objective but to deliver the praising.

A best practice is during your weekly calls or meetings with them, pull out the goal-setting document and ask questions of them on each section of the goals, looking for situations where you can deliver a Masterful Praising.

An example taken from the above document is Goal 3 which relates to the utilization of Trello. For those unfamiliar, Trello is an online project management software many companies use to assign and manage tasks while tracking the completion of those tasks through virtual "boards."

Here is the goal:

> "Utilize Trello boards more often and respond to stuff as it comes in—rather than see it and respond later (which often results in me not responding at all)."

As an astute boss, you have been monitoring these boards and you notice that the person has been increasingly active on the boards assigned to them during the month after this goal was written. You also notice they are now proactively assigning tasks to others and responding to comments and input on the boards practically in real-time. They are clearly working towards the ultimate goal of "responding to stuff as it comes in"—and although they're not quite *lightning fast* in their responses, you've noticed a marked improvement.

NOW is your time to swoop in. Even though they haven't achieved perfection yet, this is an ideal opportunity for you to deliver a Masterful Praising.

This is the foremost key to becoming a top-performing Virtual Boss. As soon as you intercept them doing something *nearly* correct, immediately praise them.

It doesn't matter if it's *exactly* correct or *nearly* correct. If it is a step towards achieving their goal, then it is highly praiseworthy.

HOW YOU DELIVER A MASTERFUL PRAISING

How to do a Masterful Praising is fairly straightforward and done in two steps. These are very similar to the techniques from *The One Minute Manager* by Ken Blanchard and Spencer Johnson—but adapted for the virtual environment:

1. Look them in the eye if in a face-to-face or video meeting. Or if on an audio meeting, then emphasize your words clearly and distinctly, telling them exactly what they did correctly in very specific terms.

2. Pause for effect. Yes, this pause is important. You cannot rush praise.

Praise intermittently, not always on every little thing. It's best to keep it a bit of a mystery as to when you will praise.

In doing this the person will never know exactly when the praise will come, so *they will always wonder when the next praise will come*. This is a big motivator. People will work twice as hard once they get a few praisings under their belt.

BE SPECIFIC

Be specific in your praise. Don't just say "nice job" or "good work." In fact, if you do it that way, then don't even bother!

Instead, be specific, like in this example from above:

> "Hey Theresa, I noticed that you are really starting to use Trello for new tasks and you're much faster in responding to comments from the rest of the team. You're also assigning tasks with due dates and keeping up with all the changes and revisions. Great work so far, keep it up!"

Notice I also didn't praise her as if it was perfect—because it's not, yet. When it is, I'd give another praising that's even more specific.

This strategy simply taps into inherent human behaviors. Simply put: people will continuously repeat activities that have been reinforced.

Reinforce the behavior you want to be repeated again and again and your team members will be clamoring for you to deliver them praise.

NOT EXACTLY RIGHT

As mentioned above, there is an important corollary to this which is especially effective for use in getting new or struggling staff members to do the right things, even if they don't get them exactly right.

If a person shows progress on a task but cannot fully complete it due to lack of knowledge or skill, *the average Virtual Boss withholds praise and approval until they get it exactly correct.*

The truly great Virtual Boss does the opposite and *praises every correct step along the way—and praises even more when it's done to completion.* If you truly want to get your people to perform without you, then here is the key!

Remember:

> *The number one motivator of people is feedback on results!*

The most important idea here is that especially when someone is just starting; catch them in the act of doing something correctly. At first approximately correct, and gradually move them to exactly correct.

MASTERFUL NOTES

One technique (which I never knew had such a positive impact until I saw it firsthand) is writing people personal notes of appreciation. In this age of email, Slack, voicemail and text messaging, nothing goes further than sending one of your people a personal note of appreciation on something they have done with great success.

Let me explain.

One day, I was at one of my team member's home office after a full day of in-person meetings. At the end of the day, I needed to go to his house to perform a periodic inventory of his supplies. As he showed me around the house, he came to his office and on a wall adjacent to his desk he had a series of shelves, prominently displayed with personal photographs of his family alongside other awards and plaques from his previous employers.

In the front center, (in a place of obvious prominence), stood an upright card that I immediately recognized as one that I had sent to him months previously. It was a thank you card from me describing to him how much I appreciated his work on a particular customer account.

He pointed the card out to me and then told me that the card from me was one of the most meaningful expressions of appreciation he had ever received. He said that it meant more to him than almost anything else on the shelves, including those awards of prominence from previous positions.

As he told me how much he appreciated the card, he spoke with great emotion. He said the card had helped him get through a very difficult period of transition both in his professional and personal life and that it would be something he would always cherish.

It was then that I realized the power of recognition and how getting people to feel good about themselves is the mark of an outstanding leader.

CHAPTER 11 TAKEAWAYS

» The number one motivator of people is feedback on results.

» Motivating your employees is as simple as praising them for specific acts of excellence. These are Masterful Praisings.

» The average Virtual Boss leaves a new employee alone expecting good performance from them and when they don't get it, they criticize them. After a while, the employee does as little as possible.

» The goal-setting document from Section 2 provides you with a 250-word document chock full of potential Masterful Praisings.

» Instead of criticizing your employees as they perform the steps in their goal setting, praise them for doing things nearly correct.

» Praise intermittently, not always on every little thing.

» Be specific in your praise—don't just say "nice job" or "good work."

» Write people personal notes of appreciation.

SECTION 3
ACTION GUIDE

THE TEN QUESTIONS

Make a plan to "peel back the onion" and get the Ten Questions answered for each one of your team.

How are you going to do it? Will it be, as suggested, at a meeting? Later this evening via email? Or live at individual meetings with each person? If you want a different plan of delivery with each person, be specific and write it down below. Otherwise, what is your overall plan and exactly when do you plan to execute it?

_____

_____

_____

_____

_____

_____

_____

_____

_____

Here is a grid you can use as a cheat sheet for the answers from your team to each of the Ten Questions (print out or save this page for each staff member you have).

NAME	ANSWER
1. What drives you?	
2. What are the barriers standing in your way of ultimate success?	
3. What are you shooting for in your current position?	
4. How do you get paid?	
5. Where do you see your career heading?	
6. How do you like to be praised? Do you like it publicly, privately, written or verbal?	
7. What's the most significant recognition you have ever received? Why was it so memorable?	

8. What are you best at?	
9. What were the qualities of your best ever boss?	
10. What were the qualities of your worst ever boss?	

STRENGTHS AND WEAKNESSES

Create a plan for each staff member to maximize their talents. Below is a grid you can use for each one of your people to outline their core strengths and weaknesses. In addition, jot down some ideas on how you will maximize their strengths and minimize their weaknesses.

TEAM MEMBER NAME:	
Strengths:	Weaknesses:

SECTION 3 - FINAL REFLECTION

Based on the previous exercises and what you've learned in this section, what do you need to improve on to be a better Virtual Boss?

_____

_____

_____

_____

_____

_____

_____

_____

SECTION 4

HOW TO LEAD YOUR TEAM
TO ROCKSTAR STATUS

HOW TO LEAD YOUR TEAM TO ROCKSTAR STATUS

One of the best speeches I've ever heard was by retired General Norman Schwarzkopf at a nationwide company meeting. The topic was leadership. He spoke about his little Chihuahua "Butch" and his Great Dane "Duke." Butch and Duke were about the oddest couple of dogs you ever did see. One was about the size of a chipmunk and the other the size of a small horse.

Despite their huge size differential, they were the best of friends. The funny thing was that you'd never guess which one of the two was the leader. Despite his enormous size differential, it was Butch. No matter where they went, Butch was in the lead, with Duke close behind.

Neither Duke nor Butch had obviously ever looked in a mirror.

It doesn't matter what size, how pretty, how charismatic, how shy, how energetic, how laid back you may be, none of these things are prerequisites for being a great leader. Rather, it takes a certain … something to be an effective leader. And looks can be deceiving. Just because you look the part and have the charisma and charm of a John F. Kennedy or the grace and magnetism of a Princess Diana doesn't mean you'll be a great leader. What matters most is how you treat your people.

In this section, I'll speak to some of these key characteristics and some specific techniques you can use to get the most out of your people.

CHAPTER 12

Lead by being led

You have much more faith in the ideas you come up with than in the ideas other people come up with, don't you?

If so, isn't it wiser to ask leading questions to make suggestions and let your team members think out the conclusion?

BE WILLING TO RELEASE SOME CONTROL

Unless they are in an absolute meltdown kind of crisis, people *don't generally like to be led* in the traditional sense of being dictated to. Instead, they prefer to be cajoled, prompted, assisted, consulted, collaborated with, and aided.

By virtue of the fact they work in a virtual business, it's highly likely your people are already going to be very independently minded individuals for the most part.

And the top performers amongst these individuals in particular will tend to feel disrespected when their bosses *assume* that they always have the right to tell them what to think and do. They'll see it as a lack of belief (yours) in their inherent abilities (which they feel are vast).

This creates issues.

There is a great trick, however, that you can use to turn dissenters into followers by simply changing the way you deal with them. It doesn't take much. All it takes is for you to release a little control and let them feel the exhilaration of being in on the business end of policy change.

Believe me, it goes a long way to getting enormous results from the prickliest of all staff members. It also does wonders for the newbies who don't know anything yet.

If you clue them in on the decision-making process, you'll start to lead more effectively in all aspects of your position.

And once you start leading this way, you'll notice your

staff are far more engaged and tuned into whatever initiative or blitz you spearhead.

It's really not too hard, but it does require certain phrasing and questioning in order to be really effective.

Whatever you do, you don't want to try this without making sure you are prepared for the eventual outcomes.

Once you give power away, it's very hard to get it back.

The bottom line is this: People love to be included in the decision-making process. They like to be thought of as important instead of just anonymous cogs in the machine.

Respect your team member's opinions and they'll respect yours. *Empower them* whenever possible and wherever appropriate. But I caution you, it cannot be done haphazardly, or it could fully undermine your true authority.

I do know this, in order to lead effectively, you need to allow others (or at least feel like they do) to *lead you*.

Counterintuitive? Yes.

Unconventional? Most definitely.

Only for ultra-self-confident bosses? Absolutely.

But effective? Hugely.

ONE WAY TO TAKE OVER LEADERSHIP OF A TEAM

When you are in a position of leadership, you definitely need to take charge. There's no question about that. How you take charge is the real trick.

Think about the following story about a leader who took over an organization in California, as reported in *Los Angeles Times*:

> "L.A. County health services boss Michael Finucane on Wednesday promised a "quick and unfortunately brutal shake up" of managers who fail to help turn the embattled department around. "I'm taking a hard look at everybody who reports to me and I'm taking a hard look at the quality of work that everybody does," he told state legislators and the Los Angeles County supervisors at a briefing on the continuing healthcare crisis.
>
> Finucane, who took over the troubled department last month with orders from the supervisors to "change it as fast as you possibly can," said he has run into heavy resistance from some workers in the agency who "think I'm a tourist."
>
> But Finucane is "committed to change." He warned that any of the top 50 managers who do not join him and meet his standards for performance could "seek employment elsewhere."

"This is going to be a very, very quick and unfortunately brutal process," Finucane said. "There are significant reorganizations that I plan to present to the board."

Later, he told a reporter that "new rules" would be explained to the workers. He said most will support the changes as the healthcare system shifts emphasis from traditional treatments at hospitals saying, "You have to give them a chance to change." Then he said of the workers, "A lot of them are going to do so. Some can't."

Now, while I understand that sometimes drastic shake-ups at organization level are required, if the above is how you tend to lead all the time, you may want to reconsider your approach. Sure, we all want to set the bar higher, weed out the underperformers and cultivate top talent, but how you go about doing this is really important.

For me, there are four places Finucane's initial statements and actions would have set his people against him from the start (thus making his job of creating the changes he felt necessary much harder):

1. Remember how, in Section 1, we discussed that you should never publicly berate your people and always defend them in public at all costs? By stating the above publicly in a newspaper I feel he immediately lost an enormous amount of credibility and

practically overdrew his Trust Account with his workers in one fell swoop.

2. From what was reported, he didn't include his people in the decision-making process for this enormous change. It's very difficult to get people to do what you want them to do when you dictate to them instead of including them (more to come on that later in this book). When you get your people vested in the decision making, they become a part of the solution.

3. By warning his top managers that if they weren't on board with the changes, they could seek employment elsewhere is quite threatening language that creates an overdraft situation in his workers' Trust Accounts.

4. Finally, making the process an "I" versus "them" situation creates a very unpleasant work environment.

While I'm sure Finucane had his reasons for leading the way he did, it's not the way I would have gone about things.

AN ALTERNATIVE WAY TO TAKE OVER LEADERSHIP

In my first meeting at a leading diagnostics company, I found myself confronted with the prospect of taking over a team that was discouraged, demotivated and confrontational. The problems were multiple:

- Operations rejected every idea presented to bring in new business.
- Service levels were at all-time lows.
- Customers were leaving.
- The customer service department was in disarray.
- Operations were actually losing product and mixing up customer results.

The list went on and on.

This was the new environment I suddenly found myself in. After having profound thoughts that I had made an egregious error in coming to work for this company, I realized I could do one of two things: quit or stick it out.

I had made the commitment to the company and my new boss, however, so I decided to stick it out.

As the day of my first meeting loomed, I thought to myself, "What would I want to hear if I were one of them?"

Standing before them, with sweating palms, I turned conventional reason on its head and instead of me telling them what I expected from *them*, I instead urged my people to tell me exactly what *they* expected of *me*. This created widespread shock and amazement as they were fully ready for the "new guy" to lay out his expectations of them in twenty colorful, yet boring and clichéd PowerPoint slides.

I had turned the tables without them ever suspecting it. I was going to start this relationship off differently than any other they had ever experienced. (I had done my homework and it seemed the previous guy was self-absorbed, rarely returned phone calls and felt slighted that he was not the one chosen to take the place of my most current boss at the time.)

As they talked, I wrote down every one of their ideas on a simple flip chart. (I have kept the flip chart paper and still have it to this day.) Their comments were as follows:

- Fight for us.
- Ask for our side of the story before you accuse us.
- Be our advocate to the other departments.
- Help us win business.
- Tell the truth.

- Get our ideas across to upper management and then approved.
- Improve service.
- Call us back when we call you.

After finally exhausting their demands, I then said: "I'll give you all those things you expect of me—now I would like you to tell me what I have a right to expect of you."

Their responses came slowly at first, but picked up pace as they grew. They were:

- Put in a hard day's work.
- Show initiative.
- Exceed goals.
- Provide fast responses on requests for information.
- Be honest.

If I had come straight in, "laid down the law" and dictated to them what I wanted, would I have gotten buy-in to my message? I doubt it.

We had made a sort of moral bargain between us. I felt that as long as I lived up to my end of the bargain, they would be determined to live up to theirs. The meeting ended with a new enthusiasm and optimism for the future and a feeling that we were all in this together. The deal between me and them had been struck.

The results were phenomenal in the coming year. The district ended the year #2 (out of 82) in the country, up from the previous year's rank of low 70s. Did the opening speech cause it to happen? Not necessarily, but in combination with other messages, it did set the tone for the remainder of the year.

Here's why: people prefer to feel that they are doing things not because they've been told, but *because they decided upon it on their own.*

When you let your people feel that decisions are theirs, they become vested in the successful outcome of that solution. They feel a part of the decision-making process. Vesting is a big factor in getting people to do what you want them to do.

TEST IT TOMORROW

People feel disrespected when their bosses assume that they have the right to tell them what to think and do. But you can turn dissenters into followers by simply including them in the decision-making process. Ask them what they think of situations you're contemplating or about which you are trying to decide on your own. Maybe you can ask them about issues that have been brought up in management meetings. Reserve judgment at the meeting and call one of your people—or better yet discuss it at the next meeting. People love to be included in the decision-making process. They like to be thought of as important instead of just cogs in the machine. Don't you?

Bottom line: Respect your team member's judgment and they'll respect yours. Empower them by allowing them to make their own decisions, whenever possible.

CHAPTER 12 TAKEAWAYS

» Employees don't like to be "led" in the traditional sense.

» Employees love being included in the decision-making process.

» Empower them whenever you can and whenever appropriate

» BEWARE, this cannot be done haphazardly. Once you give your power away, it is very difficult to get it back.

» Vesting is a big factor in getting your employees to do what you want them to do.

CHAPTER 13

The secret of "Leading by Questions"

"Give a man a fish and he will eat for a day. Teach a man how to fish and you feed him for a lifetime."

—ANCIENT, SOMEWHAT CLICHÉD PROVERB

"Give a team member a fish and they'll message you in Slack 100 times a week. Teach the team member to fish and they'll exceed all their goals and will message you only when they really need you, if at all."

—RALPH BURNS

The best bosses don't need to know all the right answers.

They do, however, need to know *all the right questions.*

The key to your sanity is to help your people solve their problems rather than you solving your people's problems. They both take time to do. But only one pays dividends far into the future—saving you hundreds of hours of time.

Should you do the work for your team members or should you teach them how to do it on their own? The obvious answer is of course you want to teach them, because you don't have the time or the energy to constantly do both.

Teaching takes minutes to do. The physical act of their job cannot be done by you, because you're not with them every day, they need to do it on their own. Don't solve problems for them; get *them* to solve *their own* problems.

The goal is simple: *get superior results from your people with as little involvement from you as possible.*

If you like receiving hundreds of Slack messages, emails and texts from all your people asking you how to do their jobs, then this may not be for you.

But if you want to improve your own quality of life and develop a group of driven, self-sufficient staff members, then this is for you. The quicker you can remove yourself as a tollbooth your staff need to pass through, the sooner you'll get quality results from your people without your physical involvement.

KEEP THE MR. FIX-IT HAT IN THE CLOSET

When your people call you and tell you about a problem or an issue *resist the urge to tell them what to do.*

Yes, I said resist.

Huh? That's insane! How in the heck will they ever know what to do then?

Very simple. Get them to *use their brains* instead of them constantly calling to *use your brain*. Ask them to decide on the best solution. Then prod them to develop a game plan. Let them set up the time frame. When the meeting is over, and the person has processed the problem, selected a solution, developed a game plan and taken ownership of said solution—you are on your way to freedom, as well as high productivity from your people.

Aren't the questions your people message you with repeated situations that come up over and over? In most businesses, people confront the same issues weekly, if not daily.

Your job is to get them to deal with their own problems and issues on their own without your involvement. Using this technique, you do things once, not multiple times.

As a result, your relationship with each of your people will not be a dependent one, but a deepened one.

By relinquishing control and prompting them to assert total ownership of the solution, they become vested in the completion of the task. After all, which will be completed better, on time and with conviction—a solution you create for them or one they have created by themselves? Remember that people usually like their own ideas better than those of others. Get them to act on their own ideas and you have created the solution with minimal effort on your part.

CHAPTER 13 TAKEAWAYS

» The best bosses don't know all the right answers; they know all the right questions.

» The quicker you can remove yourself as a tollbooth your employees need to pass through, the sooner you'll get quality results from your employees without your physical involvement.

» Keep the Mr. Fix-It Hat hung up in the closet and resist the urge to look and feel important.

» Make your employees feel important by helping them solve their own problems, instead of solving their problems for them.

CHAPTER 14
How to help people solve problems

When are you most frustrated? Chances are when something happens to you that you have little or no control over. Control is the common denominator of many frustrating events. Think about the last time you were stuck in traffic. Not only were you frustrated that you were going to be late, but you were most frustrated because you were not in control of the speed at which you were moving.

Conversely, the more you feel in control of your destiny, the less frustration you feel and happier you are at any given point in time.

The same applies to your team members. They will feel happier when they feel in control and are not being controlled. What better way to leverage this basic piece of human nature and evoke it constantly as a leader than by empowering them to solve problems for themselves?

A SIMPLE HOW-TO

This technique was first discovered in the landmark management book *The One Minute Manager* by Kenneth Blanchard and Spencer Johnson. We have adapted it here for the virtual business setting. Like the authors teach, resist the urge to answer every question with a solution, but do the following with your team member when confronted with a problem solving situation:

1. CONFIRM THE PROBLEM ACTUALLY IS A PROBLEM

A true problem only exists when there's a difference between what the *person wants to have happen and what is actually happening.*

If the person can't tell you what they'd like to have happen, then they don't have a problem. They're just complaining.

2. WHEN RESPONDING TO THEM, START WITH ONE OF THESE SIX QUESTIONS

- "What do you think is the best course of action?"

- "Would that fully solve the problem?"

- "How do you think this situation should be handled?"

- "If you did that, then would what you want to have happen actually happen?"
- "Tell me what you think you should do?"
- "How did you come up with that?"

Help people to think through the entire process of solving the problem.

Become a coach, not a king.

Remember that a coach brings out the best in others by helping them to reach down deep inside and discover their own potential. A king only gives commands.

Here's an actual example of how you should approach this with your people:

Susan: *I have a problem.*
You: *Tell me about it.*

Susan: *OK … (She explains the problem.)*
You: *So what do you think the best course of action should be?*

Susan: *I could do "x."*
You: *If you did "x," would that resolve the issue?*

Susan: *No.*
You: *What else could you do?*

Susan: *I could do "y" instead …*
You: *If you did that then would that resolve the issue?*

Susan: Not really.

You: That's no good either. Then what else could you do?

Susan: If I did "z" then what I want to happen wouldn't happen either, so that's no good.

You: Right, what else could you do?

Susan: I could combine them? If I could do "x" now, "y" tomorrow and "z" next week, I think I'd have it solved!

You: That's great.

Susan: Thanks for helping me.

You: You solved it yourself by asking questions that you can ask yourself. You're smart enough to figure it out for yourself Susan, remember that fact next time you have a problem.

Talk through their solutions. If you know they are on the right track and you know what the best course of action should be, resist putting on your Mr. Fix-It hat. If they still don't get it, start to integrate your ideas with theirs, but give them ownership by asking:

"What if you did _____? Then what would happen?"

Your goal in these situations should be to get them to take 100% ownership of the solution. If a team member has ownership of a solution, you have just increased your chances tenfold that the solution will be successful because nobody likes to see their ideas fail.

A staff member who's motivated and empowered feels good about themselves. And what happens when a person feels good about him or herself? You know the rest.

Always remember to ask them to decide on the best solution and have them develop a game plan.

First ask: *"What would your next step be?"*

Then ask them for the deadline: *"When should that be done by?"*

They have just created their own due date. A due date that is set by the team member is a due date that is rarely missed.

Bear in mind that if you fix your staff's problems the solution now belongs to YOU, not the individual staff members. And if you always solve their problems, then what about the next time?

You guessed it. They call you again.

TOO MANY CALLS

A few years back, I took over as a sales manager in a district where none of the members of the team could solve any of their own problems. They were not empowered to solve their own problems because their previous boss had not allowed them to solve their own problems.

Additionally, there was no support mechanism set up to alleviate the burden of customer service, operational or sales issues.

In my first month, on average, I would receive *no less than sixty calls a day* from my salespeople requesting me to help solve their problems. And sixty was just the *incoming number!*

Something had to change or I would go out of my mind.

So I started using the techniques contained herein and within six months, I was receiving less than five calls a day from my people.

Now, instead of them calling me to solve problems, the majority of the calls were those informing me of new business and great things *they* had accomplished as a result of their newfound empowerment!

The side effect was that morale went up as well. Why? For the same reasons I mentioned before: When people feel that they are in control and not being controlled by an outside force, their morale increases. How do you feel when you solve your own problems? You feel pretty good, don't you? You proudly say "I figured that out for myself." Your team will be no different.

CHAPTER 14 TAKEAWAYS

» Your goal must be to make your employees independent of you and not dependent on you.

» Your employees feel happier when they feel in control and are not being controlled.

» You don't need to have all the answers. In fact, you actually build trust and rapport with your employees more by not having all the answers.

» A coach brings out the best in others by helping them to reach down deep inside and discover their own potential. A king only gives commands.

» If your employees need extra help, integrate your ideas with theirs, but give them ownership of the ideas.

CHAPTER 15

How to really lead like a champion

Leadership is not about pontificating the grand vision or loftily delivering a sweeping mission statement from the king to his loyal subjects as he sits on the velvet, gold-encrusted throne eating grapes and drinking the finest wines delivered by his scantily-clad concubines.

Effective leadership is far more mundane.

It's all about day-to-day, routine interactions with your people which empower them to act on their own, take responsibility for their actions while simultaneously lending helpful insights into more effectively doing their jobs on a daily basis.

This explanation is far less glamorous, but much more realistic.

The point is that you can more effectively lead your people via solid, well thought-out daily interactions than you ever could through some spiffy PowerPoint presentation done at a quarterly meeting.

Instead of talking about it, let me show you what I mean.

Let's take the actual example from a former salesperson of mine (George) who was not consistently submitting his call reporting on time. He was an average performer, yet coachable and could possibly be a star someday with the proper guidance.

How did I approach him? Here's how:

> **Me:** I know you have had a hard time entering your call reports every day. I get reports from the home office saying that you only transmit once a week sometimes, is that true?
>
> **George:** I know, I've had a hard time with them.
>
> **Me:** Why is it that you are having such trouble? What do you think we need to do differently to get those reports on time?
>
> **George:** Well, when I get home, my spouse hands me the baby after being with him all day. Then I help her make dinner, clean up, and put the kids to bed. Next thing I know I'm so tired I just go to bed.
>
> **Me:** So it sounds like when you get home things get real crazy. Is there any other reason?
>
> **George:** No, but sometimes I start on it but then get interrupted by the baby waking up. At which point I need to go take care of him. I've been away all day so it's kind of my turn.

Me: What would happen if, before you got into the driveway, you took a half hour to pull to the side of the road and entered your calls? Then all that you need to do when you get home is plug in the laptop and transmit your calls. Would that help?

George: I think it would. That way all I'd need to do is hook up the computer and it would be done.

Me: That's right, your work is largely done and you can then concentrate on the family.

George: That's great. I'll do that from now on.

George left that meeting with a plan and the great news is, he never sent in his call reporting late for the remainder of my time as his manager.

CHAPTER 15 TAKEAWAY

» You can more effectively lead your people through solid, well thought-out daily interactions with them than you ever could through some spiffy PowerPoint presentation done at a quarterly meeting.

CHAPTER 16

How and when to use the Masterful Reprimand

As effective as Masterful Praisings (Chapter 11) are in reinforcing good behavior, Masterful Reprimands are as effective at curtailing undesirable behavior. There are huge differences in the approach for the reprimand and I'll show you how to do it exactly right.

For your tenured team members, Masterful Reprimands are particularly effective in changing ingrained bad habits and behaviors. For new hires, Masterful Reprimands should be used sparingly due to the fact that most mistakes made by new hires are made due to lack of experience, knowledge, familiarity with policies and procedures, or just plain naiveté.

If the person has been doing their job for some time and they know how to do it well and they make a mistake, be quick to respond. As fast as you are with Masterful Praisings, be just as fast with Masterful Reprimands.

Here are some basic guidelines to follow when administering Masterful Reprimands—these are very similar to the techniques from *The One Minute Manager*—but adapted for the virtual environment:

1. As soon as you learn of the mistake, call or get on a Zoom with the person personally.

2. Confirm the facts—ask the person about the situation and listen to them tell the entire story. Ask questions to create understanding.

3. Look them right in the eye and tell them what they did wrong.

4. Tell them how you feel about it: "*This makes me extremely upset because* …"

5. Let what you say to them sink in—pause for effect. Let it hurt. The longer you pause, the better.

6. Look at them clearly in the eye and tell them how competent they are. Tell the person the only reason you're so upset with them is because you have so much respect for them. Tell them: "*This is so unlike you.*"

Do it right after the mistake. This tells the person that you are on top of things and that they will not get away with sloppiness.

NEVER MISS ONE!

Unlike Masterful Praisings, NEVER miss a Masterful Reprimand. This sets the tone that you're on top of everything and not going to miss a trick. By missing a Masterful Reprimand, you lose respect and control—it undermines your ability to lead because it says to them that mistakes WILL be tolerated. This sends the wrong message and creates more work for you down the line. Do it now. Yes it's hard—it really stinks to do it—but don't delay. And don't miss any Masterful Reprimands.

ATTACK THEIR BEHAVIOR, NOT THEIR CHARACTER

Don't attack the person; separate the behavior from the person. This makes it far easier for the person to accept. It also reduces the chances of them getting defensive or blaming others. Also, don't discuss it again. When it's over, it's over (people hate to be constantly reminded of their mistakes). Only remind them if their mistakes become pathological and you are considering moving them along.

Never attack their value as a human being. Since you focus on the behavior and not the person, the staff member won't feel that they need to defend themselves.

Reprimand the behavior only.

Avoid saying "you always …" or "you never …" No one responds well to sweeping generalizations.

The average boss persecutes the person and insults their character. Your purpose is to eliminate the behavior, yet keep the character of the person intact. Be specific. The behavior is unacceptable but the person is OK.

For example, say you have a team member that's constantly late for your conference calls and it annoys you to no end and reflects poorly on both you and her. How would you approach this situation?

Don't do this:

> "You always have trouble getting on our conference calls on time."

Start with this instead:

> "I've noticed you've been getting on our conference calls late recently. Is there anything we can do about that/I'm having a hard time understanding why that is?"

Don't accuse, let them explain themselves first.

You'll find that your people will really respect you for respecting them.

DELIVER IT IMMEDIATELY

The feedback needs to be immediate or it is ineffective. Get to them as soon as you hear about the situation. It's not appropriate to save up feelings about their poor performance. This approach just makes things fester and deteriorate further. Deliver the Masterful Reprimand immediately. Unless it is delivered immediately, then it has a tendency to be less effective in influencing future behavior. Remember you are investing a small amount of time now to prevent greater problems in the future.

Whatever you do, don't save up all your Masterful Reprimands for performance appraisal time. By then it is too late. All this does is create animosity between you and the person. And it's unfair because you never gave them a chance during the year to change their behavior. How will they know for sure if the behavior is undesirable if you don't tell them?

ONE AT A TIME

Intervene early, but only ever deal with one behavior at a time. That way the team member does not get overwhelmed. Information overload will make them feel attacked and will shut them down.

CHAPTER 16 TAKEAWAYS

» As effective as Masterful Praisings are in reinforcing good behavior, Masterful Reprimands are as effective at curtailing bad behavior.

» For your tenured employees, Masterful Reprimands are particularly effective in changing ingrained bad habits and behaviors.

» For newer or new employees, Masterful Reprimands should be used sparingly.

» As fast as you are with Masterful Praisings, be just as fast with Masterful Reprimands.

» Unlike Masterful Praisings, NEVER miss a Masterful Reprimand.

» Don't attack the person; separate the behavior from the person.

» Deliver the Masterful Reprimand immediately.

» They need to hear the feedback one at a time—not all at once; otherwise information overload shuts them down.

CHAPTER 17
How and when to use "Fallout"

What happens if a team member doesn't follow through on something they are supposed to do despite all this "leading by being led" stuff and despite receiving Masterful Reprimands?

You need to act fast; otherwise they know that they can get away with it. When they think that, they will do it again and again. When they do it again and again, it will become a habit. And those are really hard to break.

Here's what you do when they don't do something: call them immediately. (Whatever you do, don't email or leave a voicemail. Better yet, meet with them in person, if feasible.)

If you get voicemail when you call, leave a message like this:

> "Hi Ron, this is Ralph, I need to speak with you immediately."

Don't mention the issue, just leave it vague.

They will call you back.

And when they do call back, ask them innocently and deploy **Guilt Strategy #1**.

> *"I know WE agreed that you would complete report X by (agreed upon date). I'm really surprised that you didn't submit it on time and I'm curious as to why?"*

You're laying a moderate amount of guilt on them here. Not real prescription-strength guilt, but a pretty nice, effective over-the-counter dose. You can amp it up as needed of course.

My point is this: When they don't do something you asked, there needs to be some kind of *consistent fallout*. Consistent is the key word here. Something done once and never again is ineffective. The fallout could just be you calling them on it and making them feel guilty for both going against their word and for letting you down.

Most times, the first call is enough of a deterrent to having them do what you need them to do when you need them to do it. But sometimes you need to step it up.

Laying heavier prescription-strength guilt works well here, ESPECIALLY if you have a great rapport with them.

My mom would do this when we were kids and, oh boy, was she ever good at it. (She was Irish Catholic after all, world-renowned for guilt-dealing.)

If they're still not getting it, go to **Guilt Strategy #2**. Say:

> "You know Ron, we've had such a great relationship through the years, and I'm really disappointed that you weren't able to complete it. I really needed it on time."

If they still don't get it then go to **Guilt Strategy #3** and say this:

> "Ron, I know you're better than this. It's so not like you. I expected so much more."

Ouch, that hurts.

If **Guilt Strategy #3** doesn't work, you may need to really question that person's character and whether they are right for the role and to be managed by you.

By "Guilt #3," 90 percent of people will fall in line with your message. If they are in that last ten percent, we'll address how to deal with them in Section 5.

CHAPTER 17 TAKEAWAYS

» If your employees don't do what they are supposed to do after you've gone to the effort of helping them solve their problems for themselves, there needs to be consistent fallout: Call them immediately and discuss live on the phone or in person. It's a four-step process:

» Lay some "over-the-counter strength" guilt on them.

» If they still don't get it, lay some heavier, "prescription-strength" guilt on them.

» If they still don't get it, bring up your doubts about how they feel about the strength of your relationship.

» And if they still don't get it, it's time to question their character and let them know you had expected so much more from them.

CHAPTER 18

Where you should spend most of your time

The average Virtual Boss spends the majority of their time with their worst people because they feel that the role of a boss is to control or direct their people.

This is one of the major reasons why the average Virtual Boss is indeed, average.

In contrast, the great Virtual Boss gives away control and power by empowering their people to think and act on their own. They know the role of the boss is to *harness the full potential of each of their people in order to help them achieve excellence.* They know "control" has very little to do with it.

Yes, in the beginning when a new hire is starting, it is wise to spend more time with them to train and familiarize them with how things are done while teaching them the ropes. But once that is accomplished, you then need to be vigilant about how your new hire spends their time.

Spending time with your worst team members or even your average team members sends a powerful message that you *validate* mediocrity!

It tells your people that "the crappier you are, the more of my time I'm going to give you."

As a parent, that's like spending all your time yelling and reprimanding one child while the other well-behaved one goes completely ignored. It's a self-reinforcing message: the more you stink—the more attention I give you.

Is this really the right message to be sending your team?

Simply put, *the best bosses in the world spend the most time with their best people.* And this is not just my opinion. Not only have I seen this work firsthand, but this fact was validated in a Gallup study of thousands of front-line managers worldwide.

There's an old expression:

> *"Feed the stallions and starve the ponies."*

As a Virtual Boss, you need to do the EXACT same thing.

SOMETIMES WHAT *DOESN'T* MAKE SENSE MAKES THE *MOST* SENSE

Perhaps you are thinking: "That makes no sense! Doesn't that mean you'll upset your best people because they'll think that you don't trust them to work on their own?"

On the contrary. Because of their continued success, your *best people are most likely your most secure and self–confident people.* Because of their track record, they are too secure in their own success to feel threatened by you. Most of them are actually flattered by you spending time with them. It makes them feel important to be thought of so highly and so worthy of your time.

Your best days are most likely the days you spend the most time with your best people.

Because top-performing Virtual Bosses understand that their primary role is to neither control nor direct, they spend the most time with their *best* people.

From a productivity standpoint and depending on your incentive compensation plan, the time you spend with your best people will yield you the greatest results for customers.

Additionally, by spending the most time with your best people you are sending a powerful and congruent message (back to the Trust Account yet again):

"You are the most deserving of my time. Further, you have proven yourself to be worthy of my time."

REMIND YOURSELF WHAT EXCELLENCE LOOKS LIKE

Most importantly, by spending the most time with your best, this allows you to witness and understand firsthand *what excellence actually looks like in practice.* By spending the majority of your time with your best people, you are *running a tape recorder in your head to remind you exactly how the job is to be done.* You are picking up valuable tricks and traits that can be passed along to the other people in your discussions with them.

This makes you a more effective and knowledgeable boss and affords you greater authority and makes you a better leader.

In contrast, you cannot learn a lot about excellence if you are spending most of your time with your worst people. The average boss would shudder at this notion. They would say:

"How can you ignore your underperformers, they are the ones that need you the most?"

And that's why they are average bosses.

On the contrary, by spending more time with your best reps, your efforts and theirs become multiplied. If you are using the techniques outlined in this book, they will become even better by you being there. And likewise, when they become even better, they produce even more, making both you and them look pretty smart.

By spending the most time with your worst, you quickly become quite adept at the anatomy of failure and how things *can't* be done.

If you spend the most with your best, the exact opposite comes true; you become even more effective.

FIGHT MEDIOCRITY AND ALL ITS UGLY FORMS

Instead of spending time with their *worst* people, a lot of bosses spend most of their time with their *average* people. They feel that if they could just get them to operate slightly above average, then all would be well.

If you are preaching the need to set the bar higher, but then validating mediocrity by spending the most time with your average team members, this also smacks of hypocrisy. Your people will notice that you preach one thing and validate another, unknowingly undermining your message as a leader. Soon enough, they will tune you out because they cannot trust you. Your message is inconsistent—which undermines your leadership and your authority.

Don't validate mediocrity by spending more time with your average people. Rather fight against it in all ways and spend the majority of your time with your best. Talent is the multiplier. If you spend the most time with your B players, you'll have little extra time to leverage the very good team members into great team members.

If you have spent ample time on "Setting the Bar Higher," then you have set the tone that mediocrity is not tolerated and the attainment of excellence is the only acceptable outcome.

Average performance is not the benchmark, excellence is the benchmark.

Paint the picture of what excellence looks like to your people. The only way you'll do this is if you witness excellence firsthand and spend the most time with your best team members.

OPPORTUNITY MATCHING

Taking the above one step further is this quick method for achieving immediate job performance impact without adding headcount: match your best opportunities to the talents of your individual team members.

If you place your best people on your best opportunities, superior results will follow. And the beauty of this is that it can be done with minimal disruption while yielding great results.

The question of how to get the most out of an opportunity is rarely a "how" question; oftentimes, it is simply a "who" question. Put the right "who" on the right opportunity and the rewards will astound you.

CHAPTER 18 TAKEAWAYS

» The best bosses spend the most time with their best people.

» Because of their success, your best employees are most likely your most secure employees and will not be threatened by you spending more time with them.

» By "feeding the stallions and starving the ponies" you are sending a powerful message to your team that the best employees have proven themselves worthy of your time.

» Most importantly, you can witness and understand firsthand what excellence actually looks like in practice.

» If you spend the most with your best, you become even more effective.

» Don't validate mediocrity and undermine your effectiveness as a leader by spending more time with your average people—spend the majority of your time with your best sending the message of "Setting the Bar Higher" with not only what you say, but also what you do.

» Match your best opportunities to the talents of your employees. Put the right "who" on the right opportunity and reap the rewards that come.

ACTION GUIDE

ASSESS HOW WELL YOU LEAD BY QUESTIONS

Using the grid below, think back to two or three incidents in the past week or month that you did the thinking for your people. Then write out how you would handle this situation without your Mr. Fix It hat and help the person solve his or her problem.

Brief description of incident	
How you handled it with your Mr. Fix-It hat	
How you would handle it without your Mr. Fix-It hat	

PRACTICE HELPING PEOPLE SOLVE PROBLEMS RATHER THAN HELPING SOLVE PEOPLE'S PROBLEMS

Use the grid on the next page to guide you through your next problem-solving situation. Perhaps make a few copies of it and keep them with you to use as a cheat sheet for future problem-solving situations.

STEP	YOUR QUESTION(S) TO ASK	REP'S ANSWERS
1. Confirm the problem actually exists	Is there a difference between what the person wants to have happen versus what is happening?	If yes, proceed to next step.
2. Ask any of these 6 questions of them	What do you think is the best course of action?	
	Would that fully solve the problem?	
	How do you think this situation should be handled?	
	If you did that, then would what you want to have happen actually happen?	

	Tell me what you think you should do?	
	How did you come up with that?	
3. Have the rep develop a game plan and timeline	What would your next step be?	
	When should that be done by?	
4. Follow up and outcome	Have they followed through on solving their problem and met the deadline?	If not, give them a Masterful Reprimand and reiterate your previous discussion
	If they have followed through, but the problem was not solved	Repeat Steps 1 – 4
	If they have followed through and the problem is solved.	It is a fine time for a Masterful Praising!

MASTERFUL REPRIMANDS CHEAT SHEET

Masterful Reprimands can be tough at first, so here is a cheat sheet for you to print out and carry to remind you of some of the basic how-to's of delivering Masterful Reprimands:

- As soon as you learn of the mistake, call or visit the team member personally.

- Confirm the facts—ask the person about the situation and listen to them tell the entire story. Ask questions to create understanding.

- Look them right in the eye and tell them what they did wrong.

- Tell them how you feel about it: "*This makes me extremely upset because …*"

- Let what you say to them sink in—pause for effect. Let it hurt. The longer you pause, the better.

- Look at them clearly in the eye and tell them how competent they are. Tell the person the only reason you're so upset with them is because you have so much respect for them. Tell them: "*this is so unlike you.*"

- Never miss one.

- Never attack their character; attack the behavior.

- Avoid saying "you always …" or "you never …"
- Deliver it immediately.
- Only give one Masterful Reprimand at a time for one behavior.

SPEND TIME WITH YOUR BEST PEOPLE

If you are not already, use the following guide to make a plan to spend more time with your best people.

First, identify the reps with which you should be spending a majority of your time (REMINDER, it should be those in Columns 1 and 2!):

YOUR BEST PEOPLE	YOUR NEWBIES	YOUR AVERAGE PEOPLE	YOUR WEAKEST PEOPLE

Use the below calendar to map out a rough schedule of who you are going to work with during the next month. The calendar should be dominated by the names of your best reps and your newer reps.

MON	TUE	WED	THU	FRI

MATCH YOUR BEST PEOPLE WITH YOUR BIGGEST OPPORTUNITY

If you do not already, use the below grid to map out the top 5 opportunities in your company/section. Who are the people currently working on those opportunities? If you identify that you do not have your top reps on each of your top 5 opportunities, which ones should be assigned to work that opportunity? What is your plan to realign so that you can match your best with your best?

TOP 5 OPPORTUNITIES	CURRENT REP	REP IT SHOULD BE	PLAN TO REALIGN

SECTION 4 - FINAL REFLECTION

Based on the previous exercises and what you've learned
in this section, what do you need to improve on to be a
better Virtual Boss?

_____

_____

_____

_____

_____

_____

_____

_____

SECTION 5

HOW TO TURN AROUND YOUR UNDERPERFORMERS IN 30 DAYS

HOW TO TURN AROUND YOUR UNDERPERFORMERS IN 30 DAYS

One of the most challenging and emotionally distressing parts of a Virtual Boss's job is to try to turn around their underperforming people.

The reality is that with every success at undertaking this venture, there will be just as many failures. And as an ambitious, top-performing Virtual Boss, failure is not something you particularly enjoy.

There are multiple techniques and iron-clad scripts that can be used to achieve a turnaround, but at the end of the day, if the person isn't producing, then you need to move on without each other, (if you know what I'm saying). In this section, I'll tell you exactly how to do that with a minimum of fluff and maximum effectiveness.

CHAPTER 19

The three rules for turning around your underperformers

According to Hall of Fame coach Bill Parcells, there are three rules you must adhere to in order to turn an underperformer into a performer. These rules are simple and effective and can be easily modified to suit your individual situation. In this chapter, I will borrow heavily from Parcells' teachings, but put my own individual spin on it for Virtual Bosses.

An underperformer may be underperforming for a number of different reasons, one of them being that they just may not have talent.

But if you have determined that the person does in fact possess the raw talent to do the job, then following the three rules outlined next will do wonders for your ability to squeeze every ounce of potential out of them.

RULE #1: SET THE TONE

Be honest with your underperforming people—brutally honest.

Tell them the truth about their performance, don't sugarcoat it; tell it to them face-to-face and tell them over and over again.

Because the only way to change people's behavior is to tell them in the clearest terms possible what they are doing wrong.

If you don't tell them what they are doing wrong when they do it wrong (remember Masterful Reprimands from Chapter 16?), you'll never get them to change—plus you'll lose credibility in the process.

Remember, when in a position of authority—take charge.

Forget big egos, don't be tentative.

Be clear with people about where they are going wrong and tell them in plain terms. When you observe underperformance, tell them that underperformance is no longer tolerated—and that if they don't change then they will be gone.

This may sound harsh, but it's not. You can do it because you have already invested huge amounts of time and effort into making deposits in the Trust Account. Now it's time to make a few withdrawals—just don't overdo it.

You can't all of a sudden become Bill Parcells if you've always led like Pete Carroll.

For those of you not familiar with these two guys, they are two of the most successful coaches in their respective fields. Bill Parcells is a multiple Super Bowl-winning former professional NFL coach and Pete Carroll is a multiple national championship-winning college football coach. Their styles could not be more different. Parcells is a hard-driving, confrontational disciplinarian, whereas Pete Carroll is a feel-good, positive-reinforcing "softer" kind of leader and personality.

Despite their differences in style, they are both enormously effective and successful. In fact, many would say they are the two most successful coaches ever in their respective endeavors. But their styles could not be more different.

All this means is that you cannot all of a sudden become a hardass if you've always led with a soft touch. You have to be YOU—otherwise, your team knows that you're not being you and you come across as disingenuous and unfortunately very ineffective.

Bear in mind, either virtual management style works.

As long as it's done GENUINELY. You need to be you. But do it so you retain control and let them know who's boss and tell them clearly where they are deficient.

Don't make it personal, because it's not.

And realistically, you're just telling them something they already know.

THE MEANING OF "ACHIEVEMENT"

As the Pro Football Hall of Fame coach Bill Parcells, says: to be effective in turning around your underperformers, you must get your group to buy into two major facts:

1. "Achievement" is the only permanent value of work.
2. "Achievement" only comes from relentless effort and commitment.

Present these concepts in a group setting at first such as at your first meeting. This will help establish your credibility as a leader. And once again, if you've been following all the teachings in this book so far, you know that in Section 2 we laid out in great detail exactly what kind of expectations you must have as a leader to set the bar higher in getting your team to shoot for excellence. Time is of the essence here, so make sure they all understand what is expected from you first. If you have not established that tone to begin with, you may have trouble here.

After the tone from Section 2 has been set in a group setting, then it's especially critical that you talk with them one-on-one.

If you have read the previous four sections, you already know that I am a firm believer that holding frank one-on-one conversations with every member of the team is absolutely essential to success. And by now, you should be a believer as well.

Tell each person what you expect of them and reiterate their goals.

You both want the same things, right? Make sure you align their goals with your goals.

Whatever you do, be very clear on your expectations.

They should know what minimum performance is. And if they don't, then shame on you and them! Shame on you for not repeating it over and over again. Shame on them for not knowing it.

Once this is established, appeal to their passion for achievement and desire to make money. However, be very clear that if they don't produce what is needed you will find someone who will. Don't make it a threat; just tell them as you would state any other fact like the sky is blue.

That's just the way it is. Tell them that you are here to "achieve at the highest level." Leaders can do everything right but if they don't set an expectation of excellence at each and every level—then they can never expect to be successful.

RULE #2: DON'T SHIRK CONFRONTATION

Make it *extremely* clear from day one that you are in charge.

Yes, continue to "lead by being led" and practice all the other leadership styles and techniques that engender democracy and buy-in. These are very effective techniques to unleash the best from your team.

However, when it comes to performance or underperformance, *there is no "lead by being led."* This is where you exert control because the consequences are dire. If they don't perform, then you need to find someone who will and they need to find another place to work.

Don't get emotional here. Do so calmly and without fanfare, but be very clear that there is little question who calls the shots.

In most cases, in order to get the most out of people, you do need to apply a certain amount of pressure to them. This pressure can take on many different forms, but in this rule, it comes in the form of frank, one-on-one discussions that speak to the heart of the matter.

Turn up the heat under your people and constantly push them to a higher level. Do this both for the underperformers as well as the overachievers.

Remember that even Tiger Woods has a swing coach. Everyone needs a push, including the uber-talented ones. Your superstars are no different.

Never forget, however, that your real job is to *elevate your people to perform at a level they previously thought not possible*. You owe it to them, and you owe it to you. If your underperformer's best level of performance falls far short, then the heat will be on and will stay on.

When you say all this, back it up, mean it. If you don't carry through, then your reputation and status as a leader suffer dramatically.

CREATE PRESSURE

So how do you create pressure?

> Coal will turn to diamond under extreme pressure. Will your team do the same?

Sometimes, creating pressure requires confrontation. Whatever you do, don't avoid it. Many people don't like *confrontation* and this is a huge problem. Sure, it gets intense and uncomfortable sometimes. However, if it is not done, it festers, infects and undermines your ability to lead others.

Think of confrontation, not as a bad thing, but rather an *opportunity to get things straight with your team.* Don't think of the word itself as having a negative connotation. In fact, confrontation is neutral in its exact definition. There is no harm in this! By looking people straight in the eye, you get to the sources of their motivation and their behaviors. Without it, you'll never get them to change the way they act.

Remember that the word confrontation should not be confused with negative criticism. In fact, confrontation is the opposite, and it should always be framed in a positive way. An example is the following:

> "I don't think you are performing up to your potential —you can do far better."

This is a line I have used on countless occasions for the simple fact that you as the boss are setting an expectation for your staff member that is higher than they may think is possible for them. You're simply giving your people a *lofty expectation to which they should aspire to live up.*

If you do this right, I guarantee you'll see results in 30 days or less.

For people whose potential far exceeds what they think of themselves (in your opinion), this is a very effective technique. In fact, it's one of the most powerful and motivational discussions you may ever have with your team!

Can they perform to that level? They may not, but regardless, you need to set the expectation that they can. If they cannot, then you'll need to start a performance improvement program.

Whatever you do, make it clear to your team that you are both shooting for the same goals. Say something like this:

> "It's in your best interest that you hit your goals—it's also in my best interest that you hit goals. You see, we both want the same thing."

Do what it takes to get a strong reaction from the person. When you have done that—you know you have gotten through to them.

The next step now is that they must be forced to act. By confronting and getting things straight you do two things:

1. You heighten your chances of getting them to the proper performance.

2. You make it clear to them exactly what you expect of them. I have always found that

people feel it is more valuable to have a manager who is clear and open than one who beats around the bush.

The best thing you can ever say to an underperformer or a high achiever is:

"I think you are better than you think you are."

Remember: manage by *behaviors* and not by numbers.

If you manage solely by behaviors, and the staff member is exhibiting the right behaviors to be successful, *the numbers will come.* If you manage solely by the numbers, the behaviors are less likely to come and the numbers may *never* come.

This is an extremely important concept for you to wrap your brain around. If you can always remember to manage by behaviors and not by numbers, you will lead your people to greater heights than you ever thought possible. Their performance will start to improve immediately, and within a month, you will see a drastic improvement in their performance.

My parents are a great example of people who were experts at *making me feel I could do better than I thought.* They pulled this sneaky psychological trick on my siblings and me all the time, and boy, did it work! The reason behind it was that their expectations for me were even higher than I had for myself. Even if they really didn't believe it, I never knew, because they pulled it off so well.

In the same way that my mom and dad did this to me, this is an extremely effective tool in extracting top performance out of your team *quickly*. Their expectations for me were *so high*, I felt that if I underperformed in any capacity, be it at school, at home, athletics and the like, if I didn't do my best, *I would let them down.*

Although they never meant to be "sneaky," it really worked well. And you want to use this same "sneaky psychology" with your people if you want speedy results.

For example, let's say I got a "C" in a class in school. My parents would be supportive, but curiously ask me why I thought I got the "C." This immediately forced me to reflect on whether I had done all I could have done on my part.

Once this was discussed, they always let me know *how well I could do with maximum effort and that their expectation of me was to do my best.* The logical conclusion was that "As" and "Bs" were more in line with what my potential was.

Another key point: they reinforced that *if you truly did your best, you could not fail.*

Your team members are no different. It is very true when I say that *people can do more than they think they can do.*

Sometimes they just need someone to show confidence in their abilities in order for them to unleash what's lurking within them. And that is your job as their boss—because when you do, you both benefit enormously in a very short period of time. If you can convince your people that they too can do more than they think they can then soon enough, what they will start to do within 30 days will begin to amaze you.

The best thing is that you can start doing this tomorrow.

RULE #3: SET SMALL GOALS AND ACHIEVE THEM

So here's a challenge for you: for those people who have the potential but have *never* performed well, after a continuous string of underperformance, it gets very difficult for them to ever imagine themselves on top.

As you confront them on their weaknesses, it's important to remember to simultaneously *build a culture of confidence and success with them.* Remember the person who feels good, produces more.

Confidence and successful thinking begets more confidence and more success. However, all this cannot be done in one contact. You need to do it one step at a time, one interaction at a time. When you continuously do it over the course of 30 days, you'll notice a change.

The important point to drive home here is:

To be successful, you have to first believe that you CAN BE successful.

Remember that only the confident person is the successful person.

This is where we would employ the "small goals" technique to get them on the right track. Let's say you have an underperforming team member who you know could meet their goals, but for whatever reason, (a previous boss, poor skills, lack of training or some other circumstance), has not been able to really gain any sort of traction in their territory.

You first need to set some small goals that can be achieved in short order, each one layering upon the next to create some upward positive momentum so that they start to feel the exhilaration of doing things right. We all want to do things right, sometimes we just need a helping hand to help us get there. That's where you step in.

So for example, your step-wise, "small goals" strategy goes from "basic" to "complex" on a continuum of complexity. Once they get the first one, you reinforce the importance of attainment of the second one and so on.

Here is an example from the old sales days of how to set "simple" to "complex" goals you can use with your salespeople:

1. Good pre-call plan
2. Good pre-call preparation
3. Good part of a call
4. Good total call
5. Good sales day
6. Good sales week
7. Good sales month
8. Good sales quarter
9. Good sales year

What you're trying to do is take them through the most basic and simple steps of their job, create confidence in achieving those infinitesimally small goals, then build on the confidence gained by those goals being achieved to ultimately get you and them at the place where you want them to be: namely at the top of the rankings.

Notice how I did not say "great" in any of these small goals.

"Great" will come later. It's most important now to recognize your underperformers when they achieve something far better than "mediocre" or "poor."

Success breeds confidence and confidence produces superior results.

Be there with them through the process, observe them in each of these endeavors and praise them accordingly. Make sure you recognize their improvement. This way, they start to "re-taste" success, one small step at a time.

Think of this process like a snowball rolling down a hill: When it first starts rolling, it's about the size of a baseball. Further down the hill, as it gains more and more speed, it gathers mass and momentum, rolling faster and faster until it's an enormous, avalanche-grade behemoth the size of a car.

Your people need this same kind of momentum building. And you will help them get that one step at a time; one praising at a time.

The sad part is that if it's been a long time since they tasted success, they may have completely forgotten its flavor. It's up to you to remind them, and bring them slowly, steadily, one step at a time back to "the buffet of success."

CHAPTER 19 TAKEAWAYS

» These three rules are to be used with underperformers you have determined do not lack talent and may have just had a temporary bump in the road to their ultimate success:

» **Rule 1 – Set the tone**

   » Be brutally honest.

   » Make the meaning of "Achievement" crystal clear.

» **Rule 2 – Don't shirk confrontation**

   » You are in charge.

   » Create pressure—your opinion of their potential far exceeds that which they think of themselves.

» **Rule 3 – Set small goals and achieve them**

   » As you confront them on their weaknesses, remember to simultaneously build a culture of confidence and success.

   » Make sure you recognize their improvement so that they start to "re-taste" success.

CHAPTER 20

Encourage baby steps

According to Ken Blanchard and Spencer Johnson in *The One Minute Manager*, small successes can be extremely powerful in helping a person start to believe in themselves.

They teach that you, as a top-performing Virtual Boss, need to catch your people doing things *approximately* right, and then praise them for it immediately in order to get them on the path to doing it *exactly* right. (Remember Masterful Praisings from Chapter 11?)

This does not mean that you only praise them when they do it *exactly* right; you will rarely get someone to do something exactly right the first time they do it.

As Blanchard and Johnson note in *The One Minute Manager*, the technique used for getting a baby to walk is the same technique you need to use to get your underperformers to perform: *You motivate them by setting small goals and helping them to achieve them.* It's the same thing with your team.

When you're teaching a child how to walk, do you stand them up, let them go and then yell, "Walk, you moron!"?

And then when they fall down, do you spank them and tell them what a failure they are? Of course not!

At first, you help them to stand by holding their hands walking next to them, and then they wobble a little and fall. You then pour kisses and hugs on them and tell them how proud you are of them. The next day they might take a small step, and then promptly fall on their bottom. You run over to them and kiss them and hug them, telling them how happy you are. The child starts to realize that the more I try this walking thing, the more good stuff I get; I wobble, walk a little and I get lots of attention. This isn't such a bad deal, they think.

The next day, the child takes a few steps until they can finally walk completely on their own and receives the same royal treatment from you with loads of kisses and hugs and attention. Pretty soon they'll walk all the way on their own.

Don't get me wrong, your team members are not babies, but they are human beings and all human beings respond to the same general stimulus, namely: **praise**.

And the wonderful thing about using praise is that it works oh so quickly, allowing you to turn around your underperformers in an extremely short period of time, namely, in 30 days or less.

Do the same with your underperformers. Praise them for at first doing things "approximately right"; maybe they asked a really good question in an otherwise mediocre call. Don't ignore it, call it out to them and build on it. Maybe they got in to see a decision-maker that a few months ago they never would have been able to see.

Praise them for this, jump right on it and recognize the "baby steps" they've taken towards ultimate achievement.

You'll soon see that they'll want to do more and more and more.

HIGHLIGHTING SMALL WINS CREATES WINNERS

Remember, when you're working with your team or on a call with them, you don't need to always focus on the actual outcome itself. Instead, focus on rewarding any and all steps *that may lead to the sale.*

Such steps can be any mundane tasks they do during the normal workday. Really basic stuff. The point is you want to get them moving in the direction of success—and through your words and actions you push them in that direction, and away from negative reinforcement and potential failure.

And remember this from Section 3: *Never withhold praise until they get it exactly correct.* If you do that, they will NEVER get it exactly correct and in no time, you'll be looking for a new team member.

With struggling team members, it is critical to accentuate the positive at EVERY possible opportunity. Then emphasize the next goal that they need to fulfill. Here's an example from my sales management days of how you may do it:

> "In that last call, I really liked how you used the targeting data in your pre-call plan to uncover the prospect's true needs. You then matched those needs with the benefits of our product. That was really excellent work."

(Pause for effect—let it sink in.)

Then say:

> "In your next meeting, what I really want you to focus on is digging deeper to uncover their true objections to what exactly is holding them back from buying."

Alternatively, you could pair the praising with a question that forces them to make the next call on what to do;

empowering them to be invested in the success of that next step.

Remember that staff always will like their ideas better than your ideas. Because those ideas are theirs after all.

An example is as follows:

> *"We really got something done on that call today—you may not have made the sale, but you uncovered needs that we can now use to seal the deal after we write up the proposal. I am very pleased with your work."*

(Pause for effect—let it sink in.)

> *"What do you feel is the next logical step?"*

The key here is to praise your people for doing things approximately correct and continue praising them until they get it exactly correct. That is how you change behavior and that is how the top-performing manager coaches his team to excellent performance.

Set small, visible goals for your team and they will achieve them. They then start to get it in their heads that they can actually succeed! When they start thinking they can succeed, it's at that precise moment that they begin to break the habit of failure and begin to create the habit of success.

CHAPTER 20 TAKEAWAYS

» Praise any and all steps that may lead to the sale, not just the sale itself.

» Never withhold praise until they do it exactly right.

» With struggling employees, it is critical to accentuate the positive at every possible opportunity, and then emphasize the next goal they need to fulfill.

» Once they realize they can succeed at attaining these small goals, they begin to break the habit of failure and begin to create the habit of success.

CHAPTER 21

When you need to make a change, take action!

Here's a big truth that you really need to wrap your leadership brain around, one articulated really well by Jim Collins in his book *Good to Great*:

> As soon as you *realize* that you *need to* micromanage a team member, that's when you know you've made a hiring error.

Yes, you need to manage and lead and coach and motivate your team. Of course.

But you should never allow yourself to think that you have to micromanage any and all of their daily behaviors.

You are not a babysitter. As soon as you realize that a team member needs to be micromanaged—take the necessary steps to move them through the process, because they will neither be a superstar nor even an acceptable team member.

CHANGE IS GOOD

Some people just need a little more help than others. But do they actually have the capacity to work independently of you? Or do they need to be constantly reminded of all the things that they should already know?

If you find yourself doing either of these things repeatedly, this is the first clue that you may need to make a team member change.

As Collins says, the big point is this: Your best people don't need to be managed. Encouraged, coached, and led. Yes! But never micromanaged.

If you hire right to begin with, motivating your people largely takes care of itself.

The truth is that you don't need to be a great motivator of people to be a great boss.

But what you do need to do is hire the right, inherently-motivated people to begin with. And if you have done that, then your problems as a Virtual Boss largely disappear.

Great scenario. But realistic? Most likely not.

Let's say that you made a poor hiring decision or maybe you inherited a person from a previous boss who is performing below expectations. Despite your best efforts, the person continues to consistently underperform. And as such, you have determined that you need to take some kind of action.

I'm sure you've done it. You have one person that continuously underperforms. You constantly complain about them to your boss, your spouse, your co-workers. The thought of them consumes your mental energy at work as well as away from work.

When you are playing with your kids on a Saturday afternoon you're stewing about it...

You think to yourself: "If I could just get them to do_____, then all would be okay."

You make excuses for them, you set up little systems of tolerability for them and still, nothing improves. Worst of all, your energy and focus are constantly on them—distracting you from spending time with your best performers.

Somehow, someway, either the person leaves or you somehow get rid of them, while your team wonders "what took him so long?"

DON'T SHORTCHANGE THEM

Think of it from the person's perspective: by waiting to act, you're also *shortchanging the person themselves.*

Huh?

If the person has underperformed for six to nine months, then there is a very good chance that the person themselves is not very happy. And might I add, you're not happy either!

As a result of your inactivity, *you are stealing a part of their life that could be better spent elsewhere.*

They could be in a place where they could be more productive and happier, but only if you do something about it.

You see the problem isn't with *them,* it's actually with YOU.

Here's another super-important point: Letting underperformers "hang on" is *even more unfair to your best people.* Tolerating mediocre performance sends the wrong message to your team AND it *undermines your authority as a leader.*

By tolerating the lousy performance, it makes you a weaker leader to your superstars. The longer the lousy rep hangs on, the more your tolerance sends this powerful message to all your people:

> "I preach to all of you to seek excellence and drive hard for success, but in reality, I actually encourage mediocrity."

I don't want to be harsh here, but it's true. Some of the best leaders have allowed themselves to unwittingly sabotage their leadership capacity by letting the hangers-on hang on.

Don't fool yourself; your other team members know who the underperformers are. They know who the weak links are. And believe me, they all talk and they know who's in hot water and who's doing well.

By letting the underperformers hang on, you send a strong message of *mediocrity* to them all, including the underperformer.

You also undermine your own authority and ability to lead because your message is *inconsistent*.

The longer this goes on the more regular, large withdrawals you are unwittingly taking out of your personal Trust Account every week they hang on, and those of your performing people.

Weak team members expect to be evaluated on how much effort they are putting in on the job, rather than what they are *accomplishing* on the job. By making clear what the outcomes need to be (see Section 2: Setting the Bar Higher), there should be little confusion.

Performance, not effort, is the ultimate yardstick for meeting objectives.

Act. Don't delay. If you know it's not going to work out—stop wasting everyone's time and take action.

As soon as you actually take action, your leadership SKYROCKETS. The powerful messages of "Setting the Bar Higher" are now being acted upon. By "casting off the weak links" the chain becomes even stronger, and you become even stronger as a leader.

CHAPTER 21 TAKEAWAYS

» As soon as you've realized you need to micromanage an employee, that's when you know you have made a hiring error.

» If you hire right to begin with, motivating your people largely takes care of itself.

» Letting underperformers hang on is sending a message that you will tolerate mediocrity.

» Act. Don't delay. If you know it is not going to work out, stop wasting everybody's time and take action.

CHAPTER 22

Why it isn't the people you fire, it's the ones you don't!

So here's the incredibly complex litmus test on how to know which of your people need to go. Make sure you're sitting down because this one is a doozie.

Ask yourself two simple questions:

1. Would I hire this person again if given the chance?

2. If this person left the company today, would I be happy or sad?

If the answers are: "no" and "happy," you have your answer.

You now know who to take action on. Don't delay. Ask yourself this question now so you can start on this next step in the process and be done with it in 30 days.

Virtual Boss genius in action, right? Seriously, this is all you need to do to analyze your team's long-term viability.

Now that you have these answers, you now know what you need to do.

SO HOW DO YOU DO IT?

The best way to get someone to leave your company is to get them to replace themselves. However, each company has its own performance improvement plan (PIP) or something akin to it. You do need to have a paper trail, and that PIP ensures you are truly giving your staff member the opportunity to improve before sending them on their way (and thus also protecting your company from litigation of any kind).

The PIP itself makes the person meet specific criteria using deadlines and tasks. If they do not achieve all the objectives in the PIP, they are given two or three chances to improve. If they fail any one of the specified tasks, they are fired.

"THE TALK"

Instead of going through all the extreme formality of a PIP and all the subsequent micromanaging by your Human Resources department, not to mention all the paperwork that you don't have time for, there is a better way. Namely: get the person to *leave on their own.*

It all starts with "The Talk."

Sometimes referred to as "The come to Jesus talk," this talk is always done in person and never by phone. A talk of this gravity needs to be done face-to-face—no exceptions. Prior to doing it, you may want to check with your company's Human Resources department.

Here's the two-step process:

1. Lay out the facts—clearly articulate to them that their performance is sub-standard; that their lack of goal attainment and track record of poor results is a large area of concern for you as well as for them. Remind them of what minimum expectations are required.

2. Then look them clearly in the eye and say one or all of the following:

   a. *"Based on everything we've discussed today, you can't possibly be happy here."*

   b. *"You have an enormous amount of talent (list them out for them). However, have you ever considered that (this company) may not be the right match for those talents?"*

   c. *"You have struggled mightily and I really want to help, but maybe the best way for us to both help each other is to part company—you may actually be happier someplace else."*

After you lay this out, wait for their answer.

Whatever you do—don't fill in the answer for them. We all have an unfortunate tendency to answer our own questions when a situation is uncomfortable (and it doesn't get much more uncomfortable than one like this).

Resist the urge to talk, let them answer and see where the conversation takes you.

Most importantly, don't be intimidated by this conversation. Look at it from a completely different perspective in that by having this conversation, *you are releasing the person from failure* and freeing them to seek a position in which they can ultimately find success.

Remember this key point: In keeping them on board *you are stealing their life from them*. The sooner they realize that their current position with you may not be the right fit, the sooner they could be doing something else more fulfilling, and yes, more successfully.

It is a tough conversation to have, but after you do have it, you'll feel a huge weight lifted—and the person will know exactly where he or she stands with you.

Don't take "The Talk" lightly. Do your homework. Have all your facts ready and waiting because there could be questions. Come prepared, be cool and matter of fact and the whole conversation will go surprisingly smoothly.

CHAPTER 22 TAKEAWAYS

» Ask yourself two questions to determine which ones need to go:

1. If given the opportunity, would I hire this person again?

2. If this employee left the company today, would I be happy or sad?

» The best way to get someone to leave your company is to get them to replace themselves.

» If this doesn't work, use your company's PIP.

» Or, use "The Talk" to get the employee to leave on their own.

ACTION GUIDE

EMPLOY THESE THREE RULES

Make a plan to start using the three rules to turn around your underperformers.

Write down the name of the staff member that needs to be turned around in the space below. Use the chart to create a plan on when, where and how you will utilize the three rules to commence their turnaround process.

Staff member name	
Where and when you will have this discussion	
Rule	**Your script (write out an example of what you will say)**
#1. Set the tone	
#2. Confrontation is good	
#3. Set small goals and achieve them	

PREPARE FOR CONFRONTATION

If you are uncomfortable with face-to-face honesty, it will help if you practice a bit before you speak with your underperformer:

1. Try visualization: using the chart you have filled in to the left, imagine sitting across from your rep at the time and place you have described and imagine the confrontation taking place.

2. Even better, role-play the confrontation with a loved one, friend or colleague whom you trust. Describe the situation to them, and how you optimally need to be cool, matter-of-fact and kind when confronting them. Have them rate you on how you do. Keep working on your role-play until you get it right.

On the next page is a "Confrontation Cheat Sheet" with my suggested phrases for use when confronting an underperformer.

Print out and carry with you or download to your smartphone for on-the-go reference.

CONFRONTATION CHEAT SHEET

Objective	Example statement
To frame confrontation in a positive way	"I don't think you are performing up to your potential—you can do far better."
Make it clear that you are both shooting for the same goals	"It's in your best interest that you hit your quota—it's also in my best interest that you hit quota. You see, we both want the same thing."
Force them to act	"I think you are better than you think you are."

PREPARE YOUR CHECKLIST FOR "THE TALK"

Use the below worksheet to help you map out the talk you need to have with your underperformer(s).

Name	
Bullets to remember	**Your Script**
• Don't take "the talk" lightly. Do your homework. • Have all your facts ready and waiting because there could be questions. • Have this file with you and be prepared to show proof and sources. • Be cool and matter of fact.	
Lay out the facts: • Clearly articulate to them that their performance is sub-standard. • Lack of goal attainment and track record of poor results and/or attitude is a large area of concern for you as well as for them. • Remind them of what minimum expectations are (numbers, and any other data that your company uses to measure results).	

Then look them clearly in the eye and say one or all of the following: • "Based on everything we've discussed today, you can't possibly be happy here." • "Have you ever considered that (this company) may not be the place for you?" • "You have struggled mightily and I really want to help, but the best way for us to both help each other is to part company – you may actually be happier elsewhere."	
Your team member's response	

Remember: Resist the urge to talk. Let them answer and see where the conversation takes you.

SECTION 5 - FINAL REFLECTION

Based on the previous exercises and what you've learned in this section, what do you need to improve on to be a better Virtual Boss?

_____

_____

_____

_____

_____

_____

_____

_____

_____

CONCLUSION

In the Introduction of this book, I highlighted that the top two struggles for all Virtual Bosses boiled down to:

1. How do I get top-tier performance out of my people?

2. How do I get top-tier performance out of my people when I don't see them every day?

The great news is, in having read this book, and being able to keep it close to hand at all times, you have access to a proven system—The Virtual Boss System™—that you can come back to when faced with the challenges and frustrations of being a Virtual Boss.

In **Section 1**, you learned how crucial trust is to getting top-tier performance out of your people. And you learned the importance of:

- Opening up a Trust Account with each of them—right from the point of hiring them.

- Continually making deposits in their Trust Accounts by:
  - Allowing them to take credit
  - Suggesting what to do rather than telling them what to do
  - Calling/video calling rather than emailing—especially in situations where things have gone wrong
  - Being present when interacting with them (yes, this is possible even in the virtual environment!)
  - Giving away your power to empower your team
  - Being authentic
  - Being a "pop-up blocker" for your team
  - Always getting their side of the story when they mess up, and protecting them.

You learned that when you go to the effort of making small deposits in your people's Trust Accounts every day, your leadership effectiveness increases significantly. Which raises the performance of your team considerably because:

- When your team trusts you, they produce for you.
- When your team REALLY trusts you, they REALLY produce for you.

Trust builds the foundation for what you learned in **Section 2**, and those were the secrets for setting the bar higher. (Not high, *higher*.)

Meaning, your expectations of your team are higher than both the expectations they have for themselves as well as the expectations the company has for them. This sends a powerful message that **you will not tolerate mediocrity** in any of its forms. This is the one area in your leadership in which you will be an unapologetic "dictator."

This doesn't mean you are ruthless, however. It means you are rigorous. If you have the right kind of people working for you, they will embrace this rigour and rise to the higher bar you have set for them. In the end, you won't need to keep being the one who sets that higher bar for them as they will set it for themselves.

When helping your team set goals that allow them to reach that higher bar, you now know it's essential to focus on the behaviors and actions you **do** want to see over the ones you **don't**.

You also need to be aware of how effective goal setting can be when using the SMART formula, while also being aware of the potential downsides and pitfalls associated with goal setting. Goals can restrain our thinking and create an effect that is opposite to the one we want.

This is why it's vital that you set harmonious short and long-term goals that are codependent on each other to decrease the likelihood of cheating or lying to achieve the goal.

Your careful guidance can help protect your employees from themselves and prevent the downside of goal setting.

Section 3 spoke about motivating your team to peak performance and acknowledged an important truth right up-front: There is no ONE way to do this. No one "silver bullet." Motivating people in a way that triggers explosive growth is the sum of hundreds, if not thousands of decisions that you make daily.

Section 3 also noted that every person you are managing is different, so it's pointless trying to motivate them all the same. They need to be motivated in line with their individual personality and needs. The easiest way to find out what those needs are is to ask them directly.

Is it really that simple? Yes, it is! Simply asking them the following Ten Questions will reveal pretty much everything you need to know about each of the people who report to you:

1. What drives you?
2. What are the barriers standing in your way of ultimate success?

3. What are you shooting for in your current position?
4. How do you get paid?
5. Where do you see your career heading?
6. How do you like to be praised? Do you like it publicly, privately, written or verbal?
7. What's the most significant recognition you have ever received? Why was it so memorable?
8. What are you best at?
9. What were the qualities of your best ever boss?
10. What were the qualities of your worst ever boss?

The other beauty of asking these Ten Questions is it allows you to make huge deposits into your people's Trust Accounts. It shows them you genuinely care about them and are going above and beyond what any former boss may have done to figure out what makes them tick.

Once you know what makes your staff members tick, it's important to acknowledge the difference between talents and skills. Talents are inherent (nature); skills can be taught and honed (nurture).

Top-performing Virtual Bosses understand the difference between these two things and push their people to be even BETTER at the things they are good at, while minimizing the things they are not so good at.

Identifying your people's individual talents and mentioning those talents in your discussions with them:

- Motivates them to be more of who they are
- Shows them you accept them for who they are instead of trying to make them who they are not
- Builds rapport, trust and respect (and thus makes deposits in their Trust Account).

You can then further boost the performance of your team members by employing the Masterful Praising techniques of:

- catching them doing the right thing,
- delivering praise that is highly specific,
- acknowledging the small things they've done right and done well on the way to achieving their goals,

as well as praising them when they actually achieve their goal.

In **Section 4**, I spoke heavily about leadership because as a Virtual Boss, that's what you are—a leader of people. In most situations, leadership involves being willing to release control and allowing your team to lead you. As Eva (whose story I shared in the Introduction of this book) found, leadership requires you to put away the Mr Fix-It Hat and help people solve their own problems, rather than allowing them to outsource all their problem-solving to you. Yes, teaching people to solve their own problems by coaching them through the process takes time. But it takes a lot less time than being the primary firefighter for your entire team.

Section 4 also covered the process of delivering Masterful Reprimands in situations where undesirable behavior in the context of the business and team needs to be reined in.

What happens if a team member doesn't follow through on something they are supposed to do despite excellent leadership from you and receiving Masterful Reprimands when they fall out of line? That's where fallout techniques come into play, and you have three levels of these you can work through.

Given it's appropriate for you to spend the majority of your time with your best performers, you need techniques for turning around serial underperformers quickly … or moving them on. As this is what **Section 5** covered in detail, these are skills and techniques you can now master.

FINAL THOUGHTS

It's easy to be a good Virtual Boss when things are going well in your organization. It's much harder to be a strong leader when things aren't going well. The beauty of The Virtual Boss System™ is that it gives you an avenue to grow and improve when things are going well, as well as a proven formula to fall back on when things are going poorly.

At the end of every section in this book, there was an action guide for leveraging the knowledge you'd just gained, along with a final reflection where you made note of where you could improve as a Virtual Boss. Now that you've finished this book, this is the time to go back to those reflections and take actions that demonstrate to your team that you have all the characteristics of an exceptional Virtual Boss:

- Someone who has the trust of the people in their team
- Someone whose teams consistently perform above expectations
- Someone who challenges and draws the best out of everyone
- Someone who sets the tone for excellence that permeates throughout the entire organization

Importantly, you now have the tools to demonstrate you are someone who is always willing to keep learning and evolving.

The Virtual Boss System™ saw my company grow exponentially over the course of seven years from a two-person team to a virtual team of over 50 people in more than 20 countries across six continents, managing a digital advertising portfolio of over $100 million.

I can't wait to see what it does for you.

ACKNOWLEDGMENTS

When I first decided to transform what was at the time, an internal training manual for my virtual teams into an actual book, I had no clue what was needed to make that a reality. After more than a year of rewrites and revisions, I now have a far deeper appreciation for every author who has ever put their life's work into print.

I have so many people to thank for helping make this book a reality, not only in how they have assisted with the writing of this book, but for all the support and wisdom they have provided me over the years.

First is a giant and heartfelt thank you to my editor Kelly Exeter. Although I was never her ideal customer (an inside joke just between us), from a world away she gently pushed and prodded me to get this book to the finish line. Despite the demands of my running two virtual businesses, balancing life with a wife and two college-aged kids, she got this thing done. To her, I'm eternally grateful.

Thanks also goes out to Kym Campradt and her eagle eyes for proofing, while Kelly's team at Swish Publishing did a yeoman's job on the cover and interior design.

A very special thank you goes to my wife Jennifer, who not only gave me the confidence to catalog my successes and failures as a Virtual Boss, but to actually document what eventually became the manuscript for this book. Without her guidance, confidence and support, not to mention a ton of rewrites and edits, this book never would have seen the light of day. I love you SP.

A big thanks also goes to my sister Mary-Carol who, as the book's very first editor, gave me the confidence to teach these strategies to other sales leaders and remote bosses. Her encouragement, modifications and suggestions helped turn the rough notes of this book into an actual playbook for virtual leaders.

A big thank you also goes to my past and present team at Tier 11 including Angela Ponsford, Mike Lambert, Tom Meredith, Deacon Bradley, Rita Ainsworth, Viktoriya Dolomanova, Alicia Katz, Adriana Cespedes and Steve Lyman. Witnessing them discovering, learning, and then deploying the techniques and strategies contained in these pages gave me the final validation that this book is desperately needed in today's business world. Seeing firsthand how those strategies have helped us build the best damn marketing agency on the planet has not only been incredibly fulfilling for me, but hopefully greatly rewarding for them as well.

I would also like to thank the many mentors, authors and writers who I have learned from, studied, and drawn immense inspiration from through the years, many of which I do my best to give credit to in this book including John C. Maxwell, Dale Carnegie, Ken Blanchard, Spencer Johnson, Stephen C. Lundin, Jim Collins, Mike Wetherholt, James O'Toole, Al Kaltman, Ron Chernow, Charles Koch, Simon Sinek, Bill Parcells, Donald T. Phillips, Bill Belichick, Jocko Willink, Brene Brown, Jack Welch, Ryan Deiss, Walter Isaacson, Kim Scott, Thom Davies, Andrew S. Grove, Gino Wickman, Michael E. Gerber, Colin Powell, General Norman Schwartzkopf, Tom Breeze, Admiral William H. McRaven, Adam Grant, Stephen R. Covey, James Schramko, Donald Miller, Eric Ries, Verne Harnish, Mike Rhodes, David Nasaw, Michael Masterson, Peter F. Drucker, David Schwartz, Neil Rackham, John Warrillow, Brian Tracy, Tony Hsieh, Marcus Buckingham, Jason Swenk, Siimon Reynolds, Richard Koch, Bob Burg and Patrick Lencioni.

Last but not least, thanks to my family, friends and everyone I've borrowed from in this book who have inspired, supported or had something to teach me on my journey. I truly appreciate your guidance and support through the years.

ABOUT THE AUTHOR

After getting fired for the second time from his corporate job in 2009, Ralph Burns knew he could no longer work for anyone but himself. With 20 years' experience as a salesperson and sales director leading remote teams, the idea of starting a bricks and mortar office-based business seemed outdated, expensive, and redundant. At the urging of his wife Jennifer, he decided to start his own virtual business.

This was done while also undertaking a two-year cross country trip in an RV with Jennifer and their two sons. It was energizing for Ralph to be liberated from the physical shackles of an office cubicle and instead build his 100% virtual business—Tier 11—from RV parks, national parks, and presidential libraries across the U.S.

Fueled by that energy, Tier 11 has grown and flourished. Since its inception in 2010, Ralph as Founder and CEO has grown Tier 11 from $0 to over $10 million in annual revenue. The company now employs over fifty employees over six continents and more than 20 countries. The digital advertising agency specializes in partnering with purpose-driven businesses to unlock their online potential.

Ralph lives in Massachusetts with Jennifer and their two college-aged sons.

www.ingramcontent.com/pod-product-compliance
Lightning Source LLC
Chambersburg PA
CBHW071534200326
41519CB00021BB/6485